NIST Special Publication 800-126
Revision 2

The Technical Specification for the Security Content Automation Protocol (SCAP): SCAP Version 1.2

Recommendations of the National Institute of Standards and Technology

David Waltermire
Stephen Quinn
Karen Scarfone
Adam Halbardier

COMPUTER SECURITY

Computer Security Division
Information Technology Laboratory
National Institute of Standards and Technology
Gaithersburg, MD 20899-8930

September 2011

U.S. Department of Commerce

Rebecca M. Blank, Acting Secretary

National Institute of Standards and Technology

Patrick D. Gallagher, Under Secretary for Standards
and Technology and Director

Reports on Computer Systems Technology

The Information Technology Laboratory (ITL) at the National Institute of Standards and Technology (NIST) promotes the U.S. economy and public welfare by providing technical leadership for the nation's measurement and standards infrastructure. ITL develops tests, test methods, reference data, proof of concept implementations, and technical analysis to advance the development and productive use of information technology. ITL's responsibilities include the development of technical, physical, administrative, and management standards and guidelines for the cost-effective security and privacy of sensitive unclassified information in Federal computer systems. This Special Publication 800-series reports on ITL's research, guidance, and outreach efforts in computer security and its collaborative activities with industry, government, and academic organizations.

National Institute of Standards and Technology Special Publication 800-126, Revision 2
58 pages (Sep. 2011)

Acknowledgments

The authors, David Waltermire and Stephen Quinn of the National Institute of Standards and Technology (NIST) Karen Scarfone of Scarfone Cybersecurity, and Adam Halbardier of Booz Allen Hamilton wish to thank their colleagues who reviewed drafts of this document and contributed to its technical content.

The authors would like to acknowledge the following contributors for their keen and insightful assistance with developing the current and previous versions of this specification: John Banghart, Harold Booth, Paul Cichonski, and Blair Heiserman of NIST; Christopher Johnson of HP Enterprise Services; Paul Bartock of the National Security Agency (NSA); Jeff Ito, Matt Kerr, Shane Shaffer, and Greg Witte of G2, Inc.; Andy Bove of SecureAcuity; Jim Ronayne of Varen Technologies; Kent Landfield of McAfee, Inc.; Christopher McCormick, Rhonda Farrell, Angela Orebaugh, and Victoria Thompson of Booz Allen Hamilton; Alan Peltzman of the Defense Information Systems Agency (DISA); and Jon Baker, Drew Buttner, Maria Casipe, and Charles Schmidt of the MITRE Corporation.

Trademark Information

Table of Contents

List of Tables and Figures

Executive Summary

The Security Content Automation Protocol (SCAP) is a suite of specifications that standardize the format and nomenclature by which software flaw and security configuration information is communicated, both to machines and humans.[1] SCAP is a multi-purpose framework of specifications that support automated configuration, vulnerability and patch checking, technical control compliance activities, and security measurement. Goals for the development of SCAP include standardizing system security management, promoting interoperability of security products, and fostering the use of standard expressions of security content.

SCAP version 1.2 is comprised of eleven component specifications in five categories:

- **Languages.** The SCAP languages provide standard vocabularies and conventions for expressing security policy, technical check mechanisms, and assessment results. The SCAP language specifications are Extensible Configuration Checklist Description Format (XCCDF), Open Vulnerability and Assessment Language (OVAL®), and Open Checklist Interactive Language (OCIL™).

- **Reporting formats.** The SCAP reporting formats provide the necessary constructs to express collected information in standardized formats. The SCAP reporting format specifications are Asset Reporting Format (ARF) and Asset Identification. Although Asset Identification is not explicitly a reporting format, SCAP uses it as a key component in identifying the assets that reports relate to.

- **Enumerations.** Each SCAP enumeration defines a standard nomenclature (naming format) and an official dictionary or list of items expressed using that nomenclature. The SCAP enumeration specifications are Common Platform Enumeration (CPE™), Common Configuration Enumeration (CCE™), and Common Vulnerabilities and Exposures (CVE®).

- **Measurement and scoring systems.** In SCAP this refers to evaluating specific characteristics of a security weakness (for example, software vulnerabilities and security configuration issues) and, based on those characteristics, generating a score that reflects their relative severity. The SCAP measurement and scoring system specifications are Common Vulnerability Scoring System (CVSS) and Common Configuration Scoring System (CCSS).

- **Integrity.** An SCAP integrity specification helps to preserve the integrity of SCAP content and results. Trust Model for Security Automation Data (TMSAD) is the SCAP integrity specification.

SCAP utilizes software flaw and security configuration standard reference data. This reference data is provided by the National Vulnerability Database (NVD),[2] which is managed by NIST and sponsored by the Department of Homeland Security (DHS).

This publication defines the technical composition of SCAP version 1.2 in terms of its component specifications, their interrelationships and interoperation, and the requirements for SCAP content. The technical specification for SCAP in this publication describes the requirements and conventions that are to be employed to ensure the consistent and accurate exchange of SCAP-conformant content and the ability to reliably use the content with SCAP-conformant products.

The U.S. Federal Government, in cooperation with academia and private industry, is adopting SCAP and encourages its use in support of security automation activities and initiatives.[3] SCAP has achieved widespread adoption by major software manufacturers and has become a significant component of large information security management and governance programs. The protocol is expected to evolve and

---

[1] Products implementing SCAP can also be used to support non-security use cases such as configuration management and software inventory.

[2] http://nvd.nist.gov/

[3] Refer to http://www.whitehouse.gov/omb/memoranda/fy2008/m08-22.pdf.

expand in support of the growing needs to define and measure effective security controls, assess and monitor ongoing aspects of that information security, and successfully manage systems in accordance with risk management frameworks such as NIST Special Publication 800-53[4], Department of Defense (DoD) Instruction 8500.2, and the Payment Card Industry (PCI) framework.

By detailing the specific and appropriate usage of the SCAP 1.2 components and their interoperability, NIST encourages the creation of reliable and pervasive SCAP content and the development of a wide array of products that leverage SCAP.

Organizations that develop SCAP 1.2-based content or products should comply with the following recommendations:

Follow the requirements listed in this document and in the associated component specifications.

Organizations should ensure that their implementation and use of SCAP 1.2 is compliant with the requirements detailed in each component specification and this document.

If requirements are in conflict between component specifications, this document will provide clarification. If a component specification is in conflict with this document, the requirements in this document take precedence.

When creating SCAP content, adhere to the conventions specified in this document.

Security products and checklist authors assemble content from SCAP data repositories to create SCAP-conformant security guidance. For example, a security configuration checklist can document desired security configuration settings, installed patches, and other system security elements using a standardized SCAP format. Such a checklist would use XCCDF to describe the checklist, CCE to identify security configuration settings to be addressed or assessed, and CPE to identify platforms for which the checklist is valid. The use of CCE and CPE entries within XCCDF checklists is an example of an SCAP convention—a requirement for valid SCAP usage. These conventions are considered part of the definition of SCAP 1.2. Organizations producing SCAP content should adhere to these conventions to ensure the highest degree of interoperability. NIST provides an SCAP Content Validation Tool that organizations can use to help validate the correctness of their SCAP content. The tool checks that SCAP source and result content is well-formed, all cross references are valid, and required values are appropriately set.[5]

---

[4] The Risk Management Framework is described in Section 3.0 of NIST Special Publication 800-53, available at http://csrc.nist.gov/publications/PubsSPs.html#800-53.

[5] http://scap.nist.gov/revision/1.2/#tools

1. Introduction

1.1 Authority

The National Institute of Standards and Technology (NIST) developed this document in furtherance of its statutory responsibilities under the Federal Information Security Management Act (FISMA) of 2002, Public Law 107-347.

NIST is responsible for developing standards and guidelines, including minimum requirements, for providing adequate information security for all agency operations and assets; but such standards and guidelines shall not apply to national security systems. This guideline is consistent with the requirements of the Office of Management and Budget (OMB) Circular A-130, Section 8b(3), "Securing Agency Information Systems," as analyzed in A-130, Appendix IV: Analysis of Key Sections. Supplemental information is provided in A-130, Appendix III.

This guideline has been prepared for use by Federal agencies. It may be used by nongovernmental organizations on a voluntary basis and is not subject to copyright, though attribution is desired.

Nothing in this document should be taken to contradict standards and guidelines made mandatory and binding on Federal agencies by the Secretary of Commerce under statutory authority, nor should these guidelines be interpreted as altering or superseding the existing authorities of the Secretary of Commerce, Director of the OMB, or any other Federal official.

1.2 Purpose and Scope

This document provides the definitive technical specification for version 1.2 of the Security Content Automation Protocol (SCAP). *SCAP* (pronounced ess-cap) consists of a suite of specifications for standardizing the format and nomenclature by which software flaw and security configuration information is communicated, both to machines and humans. This document defines requirements for creating and processing SCAP source content. These requirements build on the requirements defined within the individual SCAP component specifications. Each new requirement pertains either to using multiple component specifications together or to further constraining one of the individual component specifications. The requirements within the individual component specifications are not repeated in this document; see those specifications to view their requirements.

The scope of this document is limited to SCAP version 1.2. Other versions of SCAP and its component specifications, including emerging specifications, are not addressed here. Future versions of SCAP will be defined in distinct revisions of this document, each clearly labeled with a document revision number and the appropriate SCAP version number. SCAP revisions are managed through a coordinated process defined within the SCAP Release Cycle.[6] The release cycle workflow manages changes related to SCAP specifications and validation processes including the addition of new specifications or updates to existing specifications. This process encourages community involvement, promotes transparency and awareness regarding proposed changes, and affords ample lead time to prepare for pending changes.

1.3 Audience

This document is intended for three primary audiences:

- Content authors and editors seeking to ensure that the SCAP source content they produce operates correctly, consistently, and reliably in SCAP products.

- Software developers and system integrators seeking to create, use, or exchange SCAP content in their products or service offerings.

---

[6] http://scap.nist.gov/timeline.html

- Product developers preparing for SCAP validation at an accredited independent testing laboratory.

This document assumes that readers already have general knowledge of SCAP and reasonable familiarity with the SCAP component specifications that their content, products, or services use. Individuals without this level of knowledge who would like to learn more about SCAP should consult NIST Special Publication (SP) 800-117, *Guide to Adopting and Using the Security Content Automation Protocol.*[7]

1.4 Document Structure

The remainder of this document is organized into the following major sections and appendices:

- Section 2 provides the high-level requirements for claiming conformance with the SCAP 1.2 specification.

- Section 3 details the requirements and recommendations for SCAP content syntax, structure, and development.

- Section 4 defines SCAP content processing requirements and recommendations.

- Section 5 provides additional content requirements and recommendations for particular use cases.

- Appendix A gives an overview of major security considerations for SCAP implementation.

- Appendix B contains an acronym and abbreviation list.

- Appendix C contains a glossary of selected terms used in the document.

- Appendix D lists references and other resources related to SCAP 1.2.

- Appendix E provides a change log that documents significant changes to major drafts of this specification.

1.5 Document Conventions

The key words "MUST", "MUST NOT", "REQUIRED", "SHALL", "SHALL NOT", "SHOULD", "SHOULD NOT", "RECOMMENDED", "MAY", and "OPTIONAL" in this document are to be interpreted as described in Request for Comment (RFC) 2119 [RFC2119]. When these words appear in regular case, such as "should" or "may", they are not intended to be interpreted as RFC 2119 key words.

When a single term within a sentence is italicized, this indicates that the term is being defined. These terms and their definitions also appear in Appendix C.

Some of the requirements and conventions used in this document reference Extensible Markup Language (XML) content [XMLS]. These references come in two forms, inline and indented. An example of an inline reference is: a `<cpe2_dict:cpe-item>` may contain `<cpe2_dict:check>` elements that reference OVAL Definitions.

In this example the notation `<cpe2_dict:cpe-item>` can be replaced by the more verbose equivalent "the XML element whose qualified name is `cpe2_dict:cpe-item`".

An example of an indented reference is:

References to OVAL Definitions are expressed using the following format:

```
<cpe2_dict:check system=
"http://oval.mitre.org/XMLSchema/oval-definitions-5"
href="Oval_URL">[Oval_inventory_definition_id]
```

---

[7] http://csrc.nist.gov/publications/PubsSPs.html#800-117

```
</cpe2_dict:check>.
```

The general convention used when describing XML attributes within this document is to reference the attribute as well as its associated element including the namespace alias, employing the general form "*@attributeName* for the *<prefix:localName>*".

Indented references are intended to represent the form of actual XML content. Indented references represent literal content by the use of a `fixed-length font`, and parametric (freely replaceable) content by the use of an *italic font*. Square brackets '[ ]' are used to designate optional content. Thus "[*Oval_inventory_definition_id*]" designates optional parametric content.

Both inline and indented forms use qualified names to refer to specific XML elements. A qualified name associates a named element with a namespace. The namespace identifies the XML model, and the XML schema is a definition and implementation of that model. A qualified name declares this schema to element association using the format '*prefix:element-name*'. The association of prefix to namespace is defined in the metadata of an XML document and varies from document to document. In this specification, the conventional mappings listed in Table 1 are used.

Table 1. Conventional XML Mappings

Prefix	Namespace	Schema
ai	http://scap.nist.gov/schema/asset-identification/1.1	Asset Identification
arf	http://scap.nist.gov/schema/asset-reporting-format/1.1	ARF
arf-rel	http://scap.nist.gov/vocabulary/arf/relationships/1.0#	ARF relationships
cat	urn:oasis:names:tc:entity:xmlns:xml:catalog	XML Catalog
con	http://scap.nist.gov/schema/scap/constructs/1.2	SCAP Constructs
cpe2	http://cpe.mitre.org/language/2.0	Embedded CPE references
cpe2-dict	http://cpe.mitre.org/dictionary/2.0	CPE dictionaries
cve	http://scap.nist.gov/schema/vulnerability/0.4	NVD/CVE data feed elements and attributes
cvss	http://scap.nist.gov/schema/cvss-v2/0.2	NVD/CVSS data feed elements and attributes
dc	http://purl.org/dc/elements/1.1/	Simple Dublin Core elements
ds	http://scap.nist.gov/schema/scap/source/1.2	SCAP source data stream collection
dt	http://scap.nist.gov/schema/xml-dsig/1.0	Security automation digital signature extensions
nvd	http://scap.nist.gov/schema/feed/vulnerability/2.0	Base schema for NVD data feeds
ocil	http://scap.nist.gov/schema/ocil/2.0	OCIL elements and attributes
oval	http://oval.mitre.org/XMLSchema/oval-common-5	Common OVAL elements and attributes
oval-def	http://oval.mitre.org/XMLSchema/oval-definitions-5	OVAL Definitions
oval-res	http://oval.mitre.org/XMLSchema/oval-results-5	OVAL results
oval-sc	http://oval.mitre.org/XMLSchema/oval-system-characteristics-5	OVAL system characteristics
oval-var	http://oval.mitre.org/XMLSchema/oval-variables-5	The elements, types, and attributes that compose the core schema for encoding OVAL Variables. This schema is provided to give structure to any external variables and their values that an OVAL Definition is expecting.
scap-rel	http://scap.nist.gov/vocabulary/scap/relationships/1.0#	SCAP relationships
sch	http://purl.oclc.org/dsdl/schematron	Schematron validation scripts
xccdf	http://checklists.nist.gov/xccdf/1.2	XCCDF policy documents
xlink	http://www.w3.org/1999/xlink	XML Linking Language

Prefix	Namespace	Schema
xml	http://www.w3.org/XML/1998/namespace	Common XML attr butes
xxxx-def	http://oval.mitre.org/XMLSchema/oval-definitions-5#xxxx	OVAL elements and attributes specific to an OS, Hardware, or Application type *xxxx*[8]
xxxx-sc	http://oval.mitre.org/XMLSchema/oval-system-characteristics-5#xxxx	OVAL system characteristic elements and attributes specific to an OS, Hardware, or Application type *xxxx*

---

[8] The types supported by OVAL 5.10 include the AIX, CATOS, ESX, FREE BSD, HP-UX, IOS, LINUX, PIXOS, SOLARIS, UNIX, WINDOWS, INDEPENDENT (common) operating systems, and APACHE application.

2. SCAP 1.2 Conformance

The *component specifications* included in SCAP 1.2 are as follows:

- Languages

  o Extensible Configuration Checklist Description Format (XCCDF) 1.2, a language for authoring security checklists/benchmarks and for reporting results of evaluating them [XCCDF]

  o Open Vulnerability and Assessment Language (OVAL) 5.10, a language for representing system configuration information, assessing machine state, and reporting assessment results [OVAL]

  o Open Checklist Interactive Language (OCIL) 2.0, a language for representing checks that collect information from people or from existing data stores made by other data collection efforts [OCIL]

- Reporting formats

  o Asset Reporting Format (ARF) 1.1, a format for expressing the transport format of information about assets and the relationships between assets and reports [ARF]

  o Asset Identification 1.1, a format for uniquely identifying assets based on known identifiers and/or known information about the assets [AI]

- Enumerations

  o Common Platform Enumeration (CPE) 2.3, a nomenclature and dictionary of hardware, operating systems, and applications [CPE]

  o Common Configuration Enumeration (CCE) 5, a nomenclature and dictionary of software security configurations [CCE]

  o Common Vulnerabilities and Exposures (CVE), a nomenclature and dictionary of security-related software flaws[9] [CVE]

- Measurement and scoring systems

  o Common Vulnerability Scoring System (CVSS) 2.0, a system for measuring the relative severity of software flaw vulnerabilities [CVSS]

  o Common Configuration Scoring System (CCSS) 1.0, a system for measuring the relative severity of system security configuration issues [CCSS]

- Integrity

  o Trust Model for Security Automation Data (TMSAD) 1.0, a specification for using digital signatures in a common trust model applied to other security automation specifications [TMSAD].

All references to these specifications within this document are to the version numbers listed above unless otherwise explicitly specified.

Combinations of these specifications can be used together for particular functions, such as security configuration checking. These functions, known as *SCAP use cases*, are ways in which a product can use SCAP. The collective XML content used for a use case is called an *SCAP data stream*, which is a specific instantiation of SCAP content. There are two types of SCAP data streams: an *SCAP source data stream* holds the input content, and an *SCAP result data stream* holds the output content. The major elements of a data stream, such as an XCCDF benchmark or a set of OVAL Definitions, are referred to as *stream components*.

---

[9] CVE does not have a version number.

Products and source content may want to claim conformance to one or more of the SCAP use cases, which are defined in Section 5 of this document, for a variety of reasons. For example, a product may want to assert that it uses SCAP content properly and can interoperate with other products using valid SCAP content. Another example is a policy mandating that an organization use SCAP source content for performing vulnerability assessments and other security operations.

This section provides the high-level requirements that a product or source content must meet for conformance with the SCAP 1.2 specification. Such products and source content are referred to as *SCAP conformant*. Most of the requirements listed in this section reference other sections in the document that fully define the requirements.

If requirements are in conflict between component specifications, this document will provide clarification. If a component specification is in conflict with this document, the requirements in this document SHALL take precedence. If requirements are in conflict between this document and the errata for this document, the errata SHALL take precedence.

2.1 Product Conformance

There are two types of SCAP-conformant products: content producers and content consumers. *Content producers* are products that generate SCAP source data stream content, while *content consumers* are products that accept existing SCAP source data stream content, process it, and produce SCAP result data streams. Products claiming conformance with the SCAP 1.2 specification SHALL comply with the following requirements:

1. Adhere to the requirements detailed in each applicable component specification (for each selected SCAP component specification, and for each SCAP component specification required to implement the selected SCAP use cases). The authoritative references for each specification are listed in Appendix C.

2. Adhere to the requirements detailed in the errata for this document [ERRATA].

3. For content producers, generate well-formed SCAP source data streams. This includes following the source content conformance requirements specified in Section 2.2, and following the requirements in Section 5 for the use cases that the content producer supports.

4. For content consumers, consume and process well-formed SCAP source data streams, and generate well-formed SCAP result data streams. This includes following all of the processing requirements defined in Section 4 for each selected SCAP component specification and each SCAP component specification required to implement the selected SCAP use cases.

5. Make an explicit claim of conformance to this specification in any documentation provided to end users.

2.2 Source Content Conformance

Source content (i.e., source data streams) claiming conformance with the SCAP 1.2 specification SHALL comply with the following requirements:

1. Adhere to the requirements detailed in each applicable component specification (for each selected SCAP component specification, and each SCAP component specification required to implement the selected SCAP use cases). The authoritative references for each specification are listed in Appendix C.

2. Adhere to the requirements detailed in the errata for this document [ERRATA].

3. Follow all of the syntax, structural, and other source content design requirements defined in Section 3 for each selected SCAP component specification and for each SCAP component

specification required to implement the selected SCAP use cases. Also, follow all of the requirements specified for the content's use cases as defined in Section 5.

3. SCAP Content Requirements and Recommendations

This section defines the SCAP 1.2 content syntax, structure, and development requirements and recommendations for SCAP-conformant content and products. Organizations are encouraged to adopt the optional recommendations to promote stronger interoperability and greater content consistency. The first part of the section discusses SCAP source data streams. The middle of the section groups requirements and recommendations by specification: XCCDF, OVAL, OCIL, CPE, CCE, CVE, CVSS, and CCSS, in that order. Finally, the last part of the section discusses applying XML digital signatures to source data streams.

3.1 SCAP Source Data Stream

This section discusses SCAP source data streams only; SCAP result data streams are discussed in Section 4.4 as part of the requirements for SCAP processing.

An *SCAP source data stream collection* is composed of SCAP data streams and SCAP source components. See http://scap.nist.gov/revision/1.2/#example for a sample of an SCAP source data stream collection and its sections. The components section contains an unbounded number of *SCAP source components*, each consisting of data expressed using one or more of the SCAP specifications. The data streams section contains one or more source data streams, each of which references the source components in the components section that compose the data stream. This model allows source components to be reused across multiple data streams. Many data streams are allowed in a data stream collection to allow grouping of related or similar source data streams. For example, NIST currently distributes the United States Government Configuration Baseline (USGCB)[10] as a series of SCAP bundles. Source data streams that are similar or related (e.g., Microsoft Windows 7 content and Microsoft Windows 7 Firewall content) may be bundled into the same source data stream collection. Figure 1 shows the relationship between data stream collections, data streams, and components.

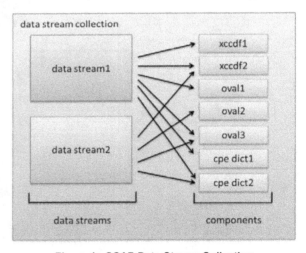

Figure 1 - SCAP Data Stream Collection

In Figure 1, data stream1 points to xccdf1, xccdf2, oval1, oval3, cpe dict1, and cpe dict2. data stream2 points to xccdf2, oval2, oval3, and cpe dict2. Each data stream is a collection of links to the components that they reference; each logical link encapsulates the information required to allow the content consumer

---

[10] http://usgcb.nist.gov/

to connect the components together within the data stream. Content authors MAY place components in any order. For example, some authors might choose to place dictionary components first to help optimize data stream parsing.

Links serve two purposes: to indicate which component is being referred to, and to provide a map to associate references within a component to other links within the data stream. The latter allows a data stream to define context for each component's references within the bounds of the data stream's own set of links. Figure 2 provides a conceptual example that illustrates how a data stream is constructed.

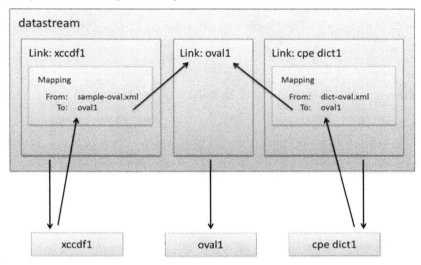

Figure 2 - SCAP Data Stream

In Figure 2, the data stream links to three components. The OVAL component does not reference out to external content, so there are no mappings captured for it. The XCCDF and CPE Dictionary components reference other components (e.g., oval1). When referencing components within the example data stream, a mapping indicates that when xccdf1 references "sample-oval.xml", the content is found through the link to the component identified as "oval1". Similarly, when the cpe dict1 component references "dict-oval.xml" the component reference is resolved through the link to the component identified as "oval1". This approach associates SCAP components within a data stream at the SCAP logical level, allowing components to be reused across data streams within the same data stream collection. This reuse can be accomplished irrespective of how references are made within a given component.

The following is a stripped down example of the source data stream. The details are covered later in this specification.

```
<ds:data-stream-collection id="dsc1" schematron-version="1.0">
 <ds:data-stream id="ds1" scap-version="1.2" use-case="CONFIGURATION">
   <ds:dictionaries>
     <ds:component-ref id="ref1" xlink:href="#dict1">
       <cat:catalog>
         <cat:uri name="dict-oval.xml" uri="#ref3"/>
       </cat:catalog>
     </ds:component-ref>
   </ds:dictionaries>
   <ds:checklists>
     <ds:component-ref id="ref2" xlink:href="#xccdf1">
       <cat:catalog>
         <cat:uri name="sample-oval.xml" uri="#ref3"/>
```

11

```
        </cat:catalog>
      </ds:component-ref>
    </ds:checklists>
    <ds:checks>
      <ds:component-ref id="ref3" xlink:href="#oval1"/>
    </ds:checks>
  </ds:data-stream>
  <ds:component id="xccdf1">
    <xccdf:Benchmark>
      <xccdf:Rule>
        <xccdf:check system="http://oval.mitre.org/XMLSchema/oval-definitions-5">
          <xccdf:check-content-ref href="sample-oval.xml" name="oval:gov.nist:def:1"/>
        </xccdf:check>
      </xccdf:Rule>
    </xccdf:Benchmark>
  </ds:component>
  <ds:component id="oval1">
    <oval-def:oval_definitions>...</oval-def:oval_definitions>
  </ds:component>
  <ds:component id="dict1">
    <cpe2-dict:cpe-list>
      <cpe2-dict:cpe-item name="cpe:/a:oracle:database_server:11.1.0.6.0::enterprise">
        <cpe2-dict:check href="dict-oval.xml"
          system="http://oval.mitre.org/XMLSchema/oval-definitions-5>
          oval:gov.nist:def:2</cpe2-dict:check>
        <cpe2-dict-ext:cpe23-item
          name="cpe:2.3:a:oracle:database_server:11.1.0.6.0:-:-:-:enterprise:-:-:-"/>
      </cpe2-dict:cpe-item>
    </cpe2-dict:cpe-list>
  </ds:component>
</ds:data-stream-collection>
```

The design of the SCAP source data stream is important for the following reasons:

1. Individual components may be developed outside of an SCAP data stream where the binding to other components is not necessarily known at the time the component is created.

2. The SCAP source data stream creates a binding between different components that were not necessarily designed to reference each other. For example, XCCDF was not designed to reference a particular checking system; it can reference OVAL, OCIL, and other checking systems.

3. The logical link mapping in the data stream places a layer of capability within the data stream to control the dereferencing of URIs within components, creating a complete solution related to bundling components.

4. The SCAP source data stream format will be useful in future communication models such as web services, transport protocols, tasking mechanisms, etc.

5. The SCAP source data stream format supports more comprehensive validation of component content, including interrelationships between components.

3.1.1 Source Data Stream Data Model

The tables in this section formalize the SCAP source data stream data model. The tables contain requirements and MUST be interpreted as follows:

- The "Element Name" field indicates the name for the XML element being described. Each element name has a namespace prefix indicating the namespace to which the element belongs. See Table 1 for a mapping of namespace prefixes to namespaces.

- The "Element Definition" field indicates the prose description of the element. The definition field MAY contain key words as indicated in [RFC2119].

- The "Properties" field is broken into four subfields:

  o The "Name" column indicates the name of a property that MAY, SHOULD, or MUST be included in the described element, in accordance with the cardinality indicated in the "Count" column and any [RFC2119] requirement words in the "Property Definition" column.

  o The "Type" column indicates the REQUIRED data type for the value of the property. There are two categories of types: literal and element. A literal type indicates the type of literal as defined in [XMLS]. An element type references the name of another element that ultimately defines that property.

  o The "Count" column indicates the cardinality of the property within the element. The property MUST be included in the element in accordance with the cardinality. If a range is given, and "n" is the upper bound of the range, then the upper limit SHALL be unbounded.

  o The "Property Definition" column defines the property in the context of the element. The definition MAY contain key words as indicated in [RFC2119].

Table 2 - ds:data-stream-collection

Element Name: ds:data-stream-collection			
Element Definition	The top-level element for a SCAP data stream collection. It contains the data streams and components that comprise this data stream collection, along with any data stream signatures.		
Properties:			
Name	Type	Count	Property Definition
id	literal – ID	1	The identifier for the data stream collection. This identifier MUST be globally unique (see Section 3.1.3).
schematron-version	literal – token	1	The version of the SCAP Requirements Schematron rule set to which the data stream collection conforms.
data-stream	element – ds:data-stream	1-n	An element that represents a single data stream (see Table 3).
component	element – ds:component	1-n	An element that represents content expressed using an SCAP component specification (see Table 10).
extended-component	element – ds:extended-component	0-n	An element that holds non-SCAP components to enable extension (see Table 11).
Signature	element – dsig:Signature	0-n	An XML digital signature element. Sections 3.10 and 4.8 define the requirements for this element.

Table 3 - ds:data-stream

Element Name: ds:data-stream			
Element Definition	A data stream. This element contains the links to all of the components that comprise this data stream.		
Properties			
Name	Type	Count	Property Definition
id	literal – ID	1	The identifier for the data stream. This identifier MUST be globally unique (see Section 3.1.3).

use-case	literal – token	1	The use case represented by the data stream. The value MUST be one of the following: CONFIGURATION, VULNERABILITY, INVENTORY, or OTHER. The value selected MUST indicate which type of content is being represented as defined in Section 5. The value "OTHER" is for content that does not correspond to a specific use case; this content MUST be valid according to the requirements defined in Sections 3 and 4.
scap-version	literal – token	1	The targeted SCAP version. The value MUST be 1.2, 1.1, or 1.0. The value MUST indicate which version of SCAP the content is conformant with. 1.2 MUST be specified to be conformant with this version of SCAP.
timestamp	literal – dateTime	0-1	The date and time when this data stream was created.
dictionaries	element – ds:dictionaries	0-1	Links to dictionary components (see Table 4).
checklists	element – ds:checklists	0-1	Links to checklist components (see Table 5).
checks	element – ds:checks	1	Links to check components (see Table 6).
extended-components	element – ds:extended-components	0-1	Links to non-standard components (see Table 7). See Section 4.2 for information on processing this element.

Table 4 - ds:dictionaries

Element Name: ds:dictionaries			
Element Definition	A container element that holds references to one or more dictionary components.		
Properties			
Name	**Type**	**Count**	**Property Definition**
component-ref	element – component-ref	1-n	MUST contain a reference to a dictionary component (a component containing CPE dictionary content).

Table 5 - ds:checklists

Element Name: ds:checklists			
Element Definition	A container element that holds references to one or more checklists.		
Properties			
Name	**Type**	**Count**	**Property Definition**
component-ref	element – component-ref	1-n	MUST contain a reference to a checklist component (a component containing an `<xccdf:Benchmark>` or an `<xccdf:Tailoring>` element).

14

Table 6 - ds:checks

Element Name: ds:checks			
Element Definition	A container element that holds references to one or more check components.		
Properties			
Name	**Type**	**Count**	**Property Definition**
component-ref	element – component-ref	1-n	MUST contain a reference to a check component (a component containing check content). See Section 3.2.4.2 for information on SCAP check system support and requirements.

Table 7 - ds:extended-components

Element Name: ds:extended-components			
Element Definition	A container element that holds references to one or more extended components for the SCAP data stream, including non-standard components.		
Properties			
Name	**Type**	**Count**	**Property Definition**
component-ref	element – component-ref	1-n	MUST contain a reference to a non-standard component (a `<ds:extended-component>` element). See Table 11.

Table 8 - ds:component-ref

Element Name: ds:component-ref			
Element Definition	An element that encapsulates the information necessary to link to a component within the data stream collection, or to external content, which gives context to the reference. This is a simple XLink [XLINK].		
Properties			
Name	**Type**	**Count**	**Property Definition**
id	literal - ID	1	The identifier for the reference. This identifier MUST be globally unique (see Section 3.1.3).
type	literal – xlink:type	0-1	The type of XLink represented. The `<ds:component-ref>` is constrained to a simple XLink, so the value of this field MUST be 'simple' if specified.
href	literal – xlink:href	1	A URI to the target component (either local to the data stream collection or remote). When referencing a local component, the URI MUST be in the form '#' + componentId (e.g. "#component1"). When referencing external content, the URI MUST dereference to an XML stream representing the content of the target component.
catalog	element – cat:catalog	0-1	An XML Catalog that defines the mapping between external URI links in the component being referenced by this `<ds:component-ref>`, and where those URIs should map to within the context of this data stream. See Table 9.

Table 9 – cat:catalog

Element Name: cat:catalog	
Element Definition	A catalog element defined by the OASIS XML Catalog specification [XMLCAT]. Within an SCAP source data stream this element SHALL contain one or more `<cat:uri>` and/or `<cat:rewriteURI>` elements, and it SHALL NOT contain any other elements or attributes. Refer to Section 7 of [XMLCAT] for information on determining which catalog entry to apply.

Properties

Name	Type	Count	Property Definition
uri	element – cat:uri	0-n (at least 1 of this or rewriteURI MUST be provided)	Maps a reference in the enclosing `<ds:component-ref>` element's component to some other `<ds:component-ref>` element that MUST be used to resolve the reference.[11] A `<cat:uri>` element SHALL have a `@name` attribute and a `@uri` attribute. The `@name` attribute is the source of the mapping, and the `@uri` attribute is the destination of the mapping. The `@name` attr bute MUST contain a URI that matches a "referenced URI" in the data stream component referenced by the `<ds:component-ref>` that holds this element. The "referenced URI" is a URI entry defined within the model used within the data stream component. The `@uri` attribute MUST be populated with the value "#" + `@id` of a `<ds:component-ref>`. When resolving the URI in the `@name` attribute, the `<ds:component-ref>` pointed to by the `@uri` attribute SHALL be used.
rewriteURI	element – cat:rewriteURI	0-n (at least 1 of this or uri MUST be provided)	SHALL have a `@uriStartString` attr bute and a `@rewritePrefix` attribute specified. The `@uriStartString` attr bute SHALL be populated with the start of a URI of an external link specified within the component referenced by this element's enclosing `<ds:component-ref>` element that is to be replaced. The `@rewritePrefix` attribute SHALL be populated with a string that will replace the matched `@uriStartString` value. The resulting URI MUST be used to resolve the link. See [XMLCAT] for more details.

Table 10 – ds:component

Element Name: ds:component	
Element Definition	A container for a single component. The types of components are defined in Section 3.1.2.

Properties

Name	Type	Count	Property Definition
id	literal – ID	1	The identifier for the component. This identifier MUST be globally unique (see Section 3.1.3).
timestamp	literal – dateTime	1	Indicates when the `<ds:component>` was created or last updated.
Benchmark	element – xccdf:Benchmark		XCCDF benchmark
oval_definitions	element – oval-def:oval_definitions	1, and only 1, of these elements	OVAL Definitions
ocil	element – ocil:ocil		OCIL questionnaire
cpe-list	element – cpe2-dict:cpe-list		CPE dictionary
Tailoring	element – xccdf:Tailoring		XCCDF tailoring

---

[11] See http://scap.nist.gov/revision/1.2/#resources for an example of `<cat:uri>`.

Table 11 – ds:extended-component

Element Name: ds:extended-component			
Element Definition	This element holds content that does not fit within the other defined component types descr bed in Table 10. Authors SHOULD use this element as an extension point to capture content that is not captured in a regular component. The content of this element SHALL be an XML element in a namespace other than the SCAP source data stream namespace. Linking through a `<ds:extended-component>` element SHALL make the data stream non-conformant with SCAP.		
Properties			
Name	**Type**	**Count**	**Property Definition**
id	literal – ID	1	The identifier for the component. This identifier MUST be globally unique (see Section 3.1.3).
timestamp	literal – dateTime	1	Indicates when the `<ds:extended-component>` was created or last updated.

3.1.2 Source Data Stream Collection Validation

The SCAP source data stream collection SHALL validate against the XML schema representation for the source data stream, as well as all Schematron rules embedded within that schema. The SCAP components referenced by each `<ds:component>` and `<ds:extended-component>` element SHALL validate against the corresponding component schema and its embedded Schematron rules. All of the SCAP-related schemas are referenced at http://scap.nist.gov/revision/1.2/#schema. See Table 22 in Appendix C for a list of SCAP component schema and Schematron file locations.

Each SCAP source data stream component SHALL use one of the elements specified in Table 12 as its document element. Each SCAP source data stream component SHOULD NOT use any constructs that are deprecated in its associated specification. While Section 4.1 requires that products support deprecated constructs, these constructs should be avoided to minimize the impact to content use when these constructs are removed from future revisions of the associated specifications. Any component in a data stream collection SHALL be referenced not more than once by any data stream in that collection.

Table 12 - SCAP Source Data Stream Component Document Elements

Component	Document Element
XCCDF Benchmark	`<xccdf:Benchmark>`
XCCDF Tailoring	`<xccdf:Tailoring>`
OVAL	`<oval-def:oval_definitions>`
OCIL	`<ocil:ocil>`
CPE Dictionary	`<cpe2-dict:cpe-list>`

NIST provides an SCAP Content Validation Tool, which is designed to help validate the correctness of SCAP data streams.[12] The SCAP Content Validation Tool is a command-line tool that will check that SCAP source and result content is well-formed, cross references are valid, and required values are appropriately set. Errors and warnings are returned in both XML and Hypertext Markup Language (HTML) formats. Validation of each SCAP source data stream component SHALL be done in accordance with the portions of this document that define requirements for the associated component specification.

If applicable, each component MUST validate against its associated Schematron stylesheet. For the SCAP source data stream collection, it MUST validate against the version of the SCAP Schematron rules as specified on the `<ds:data-stream-collection>` element's `@schematron-version` attribute, and it SHOULD also validate against the latest Schematron rules. NIST provides and maintains a set of

---

[12] The tool can be downloaded from http://scap.nist.gov/revision/1.2/#tools.

Schematron rules to check well-formed SCAP content. The Schematron files for the SCAP specification and its applicable component specifications are located at http://scap.nist.gov/revision/1.2/#schematron. Source content SHOULD pass all Schematron assertions in the Schematron rule files. When creating source content, failed assertions with a "warning" flag MAY be disregarded if the assertion discovers an issue in the content that is justifiable and expected based on the needs of the content author. When executing source content, all failed assertions with a "warning" flag MUST be disregarded.

The Schematron rule sets are interpretations of the specifications, and the implementations of their rules are subject to change. Whenever a change is made to a Schematron file, the SCAP errata document will be updated and the new Schematron file will be posted. The latest Schematron file SHOULD be used in place of any earlier versions. If the latest file is unavailable, the version specified on the `<ds:data-stream-collection>` element's `@schematron-version` attribute SHALL be used instead. Also, for the component specifications, the Schematron file on the SCAP website SHALL be used in place of any corresponding Schematron file available elsewhere. For example, a particular specification may have an official Schematron file available on a different website. In most cases, the copy on the SCAP website will be the same, but if issues in a Schematron file are discovered, the SCAP website may address these before the individual specification's maintainers do.

3.1.3 Globally Unique Identifiers

The elements listed in Table 13 have special conventions around the format of their identifiers (`@id` attribute). Authors MUST follow these conventions because they preserve the global uniqueness of the resulting identifiers. In Table 13, *namespace* contains a valid reverse-DNS style string (limited to letters, numbers, periods, and the hyphen character) that is associated with the content author. Examples include "com.acme.finance" and "gov.tla". These namespace strings MAY have any number of parts, and SCAP content consumers processing them SHALL treat them as case-insensitive (e.g., com.ABC is considered identical to com.abc). The *name* in the format conventions MUST be an NCName-compliant string [XMLS].

Table 13 – Element Identifier Format Convention

Element	Identifier Format Convention
`<ds:data-stream-collection>`	scap_*namespace*_collection_*name*
`<ds:data-stream>`	scap_*namespace*_datastream_*name*
`<ds:component-ref>`	scap_*namespace*_cref_*name*
`<ds:component>`	scap_*namespace*_comp_*name*
`<ds:extended-component>`	scap_*namespace*_ecomp_*name*

3.2 Extensible Configuration Checklist Description Format (XCCDF)

This section lists requirements and recommendations for using the Extensible Configuration Checklist Description Format (XCCDF) to express an XCCDF benchmark or tailoring component of an SCAP source data stream (see Table 12). They are organized by the following categories: general, `<xccdf:Benchmark>`, `<xccdf:Profile>`, `<xccdf:Rule>`, `<xccdf:Value>`, and `<xccdf:Group>`.

3.2.1 General

The `@xml:base` attribute SHALL NOT be allowed in XCCDF content. This attribute is not compatible with the SCAP data stream model.

Descriptive information within XCCDF MAY be used by SCAP products to assist in the selection of the appropriate SCAP data stream, ensure that the most recent or correct version of an XCCDF document is used, and provide additional information about the document. The following requirements and conventions apply to the *<xccdf:Benchmark>*, *<xccdf:Profile>*, *<xccdf:Value>*, *<xccdf:Group>*, and *<xccdf:Rule>* elements:

1. One or more instances of the *<xccdf:title>* element SHALL be provided. Each instance MUST contain a text value that briefly indicates the purpose of the containing element.

2. One or more instances of the *<xccdf:description>* element SHALL be provided. Each instance MUST contain a text value that describes the purpose of the containing element.

XInclude elements SHALL NOT be included in XCCDF content [XINCLUDE].

All remaining OPTIONAL elements in the XCCDF schema MAY be included at the author's discretion unless otherwise noted in this document.

3.2.2 The <xccdf:Benchmark> Element

The following requirements and recommendations apply to the *<xccdf:Benchmark>* element:

1. The *<xccdf:version>* element and the *@id* attribute SHALL be used together to uniquely identify all revisions of a benchmark.
   a. Multiple revisions of a single benchmark SHOULD have the same *@id* attribute value and different *<xccdf:version>* element values, so that someone who reviews the revisions can readily identify them as multiple versions of a single benchmark.
   b. Multiple revisions of a single benchmark SHOULD have *<xccdf:version>* element values that indicate the revision sequence, so that the history of changes from the original benchmark can be determined.
   c. The *@time* attribute of the *<xccdf:version>* element SHOULD be used for a timestamp of when the benchmark was defined.

2. The *@update* attribute of the *<xccdf:version>* element SHOULD be used for a URI that specifies where updates to the benchmark can be obtained.

3. The *<xccdf:Benchmark>* element SHALL have an *@xml:lang* attribute.

4. The *@style* attribute SHOULD have the value "SCAP_1.2".

5. The *<xccdf:status>* element SHALL indicate the current status of the benchmark document. The associated text value SHALL be "draft" for documents released in public draft state and "accepted" for documents that have been officially released by an organization. The *@date* attribute SHALL be populated with the date of the status change. Additional *<xccdf:status>* elements MAY be included to indicate historic status transitions.

6. The *<xccdf:metadata>* element SHALL be provided and SHALL, at minimum, contain the Dublin Core [DCES] terms from Table 14. If provided, additional Dublin Core terms SHALL follow the required terms within the element sequence.

Table 14 - Use of Dublin Core Terms in <xccdf:metadata>

Dublin Core Term	Description of Use
`<dc:creator>`	The person, organization, and/or service that created the benchmark
`<dc:publisher>`	The person, organization, and/or service that published the benchmark
`<dc:contributor>`	The person, organization, and/or service that contributed to the creation of the benchmark
`<dc:source>`	An identifier that indicates the organizational context of the benchmark's *@id* attribute. An organizationally specific URI SHOULD be used.

3.2.3 The <xccdf:Profile> Element

As stated in the XCCDF specification, the use of an *<xccdf:Profile>* element is not required. SCAP content commonly includes *<xccdf:Profile>* elements, so people tend to assume that they are required, but they are optional.

Use of the *<xccdf:set-complex-value>* element within the *<xccdf:Profile>* element SHALL NOT be allowed.

3.2.4 The <xccdf:Rule> Element

The following requirements and recommendations apply to the *<xccdf:Rule>* element. The topics they address are *<xccdf:ident>* elements, *<xccdf:check>* elements, patches up-to-date rules, and CVSS and CCSS scores.

3.2.4.1 The <xccdf:ident> Element

Each *<xccdf:Rule>* element SHALL include an *<xccdf:ident>* element containing a CVE, CCE, or CPE identifier reference if an appropriate identifier exists. The meaning of the identifier MUST be consistent with the recommendation implemented by the *<xccdf:Rule>* element. If the rule references an OVAL Definition, then *<xccdf:ident>* element content SHALL match the corresponding CVE, CCE, or CPE identifier found in the associated OVAL Definition(s) if an appropriate identifier exists and if that OVAL Definition is the only input to the rule's final result.

When referencing a CVE, CCE, or CPE identifier, an *<xccdf:Rule>* element MUST have a purpose consistent with one of the rows in Table 15. Based on the purpose of the *<xccdf:Rule>* element, the *<xccdf:Rule>* SHALL define its *<xccdf:ident>* element's *@system* attribute using the corresponding value from Table 15. Also, if the *<xccdf:Rule>* element references an OVAL Definition, it SHALL reference an OVAL Definition of the specified class.

Table 15 – <xccdf:Rule> and <xccdf:ident> Element Values

Purpose of the <xccdf:Rule>	OVAL Definition Class	Identifier Type	Value for <xccdf:ident> @system attribute
Check compliance with a configuration setting	compliance	CCE	http://cce.mitre.org
Perform a software inventory check	inventory	CPE	http://cpe.mitre.org
Check for a software flaw vulnerability	vulnerability	CVE	http://cve.mitre.org

Here is a partial example of a rule intended to check compliance with a configuration setting:

```
<xccdf:Rule id="xccdf_gov.nist.fdcc.xp_value_AuditAccountLogonEvents">
    ...
    <xccdf:ident system="http://cce.mitre.org">CCE-3867-0</xccdf:ident>
    ...
</xccdf:Rule>
```

See Section 4.5.1 for information on the meaning of a "pass/fail" rule result relating to each of the identifier types in Table 15. All rules that contain CCE, CPE, or CVE entries in their `<xccdf:ident>` elements MUST obey these meanings. As a result, such `<xccdf:ident>` elements MUST only be included either if the recommendation is identical to these associated meanings or if they have a `@con:negate` attribute (as described in Section 4.5.1) set to comply with the intended meaning (by default, `@con:negate` is set to false). In SCAP, an `<xccdf:ident>` element is not simply a reference to related material – it is a declaration of exact alignment with the described meanings.

An `<xccdf:ident>` element referencing a CVE, CCE, or CPE identifier SHALL be ordered before other `<xccdf:ident>` elements referencing non-SCAP identifiers. Identifiers from previous revisions of CCE or CPE MAY also be specified following the SCAP identifiers.

3.2.4.2 The <xccdf:check> Element

The following requirements and recommendations apply to the `<xccdf:check>` element:

1. The `<xccdf:check-content>` element SHALL NOT be used to embed check content directly into XCCDF content.

2. At least one `<xccdf:check-content-ref>` element MUST be provided for each `<xccdf:check>` element.

3. When evaluating an `<xccdf:check-content-ref>` element within an `<xccdf:check>` element, its `@href` attribute either MUST contain a "#" + `@id` of a `<ds:component-ref>` element or MUST be resolved in the context of the XML Catalog specified as part of the `<ds:component-ref>` element that is referencing this benchmark. In either case, the `@href` attribute MUST ultimately resolve to a `<ds:component-ref>` element in the data stream referencing the benchmark containing this `<xccdf:check-content-ref>` element. See Section 3.1.1 for additional information on `<ds:component-ref>` resolution.

This version of SCAP supports the OVAL and OCIL check systems. Use of these check systems SHALL be restricted as follows:

1. OVAL check system
    i. Use of the OVAL check system SHALL be indicated by setting the `<xccdf:check>` element's `@system` attribute to "`http://oval.mitre.org/XMLSchema/oval-definitions-5`".
    ii. The `@href` attribute in the `<xccdf:check-content-ref>` element MUST reference an OVAL source data stream component using the `<ds:component-ref>` approach defined above.
    iii. Use of the `@name` attribute in the `<xccdf:check-content-ref>` element is OPTIONAL. If present, it MUST reference an OVAL Definition in the designated OVAL source data stream component, otherwise see Section 4.5.2 for information on use of the `@multi-check` attribute.

2. OCIL check system
    i. OCIL questionnaires SHOULD NOT be used if OVAL can perform the same check correctly.
    ii. Use of the OCIL check system SHALL be indicated by setting the `<xccdf:check>` element's `@system` attribute to "`http://scap.nist.gov/schema/ocil/2`".
    iii. The `@href` attribute in the `<xccdf:check-content-ref>` element MUST reference an OCIL source data stream component using the `<ds:component-ref>` approach defined above.

21

iv. Use of the `@name` attribute in the `<xccdf:check-content-ref>` element is OPTIONAL. If present, it MUST reference an OCIL questionnaire in the designated OCIL source data stream component, otherwise see Section 4.5.2 for information on use of the `@multi-check` attribute.

v. Follow the additional requirements in Appendix B of NIST Interagency Report (IR) 7692, *Specifications for the Open Checklist Interactive Language (OCIL) Version 2.0* [OCIL].

If a check system that is not supported by SCAP is used in XCCDF content, this content SHALL NOT be considered well-formed with regards to SCAP.

3.2.4.3 Use of a Patches Up-To-Date Rule

An OVAL source data stream component MAY be used to represent a series of checks to verify that patches have been installed. Historically, an XCCDF convention has been used to identify such a reference. An XCCDF benchmark MAY include a patches up-to-date rule that MUST reference an OVAL source data stream component. When implementing a patches up-to-date XCCDF rule, the following approach SHALL be used:

1. The source data stream MUST include the OVAL source data stream component referenced by the patches up-to-date rule, which contains one or more OVAL patch class definitions.

2. The `<xccdf:Rule>` element that references an OVAL source data stream component SHALL have the `@id` attribute value of "*xccdf_NAMESPACE_rule_security_patches_up_to_date*", where *NAMESPACE* is the reverse DNS format namespace associated with the content maintainer.

3. Each `<xccdf:check-content-ref>` element SHALL omit the `@name` attribute.

4. The `@multi-check` attribute of the `<xccdf:check>` element SHOULD be set to "true". This causes a separate `<xccdf:rule-result>` to be generated for each OVAL Definition. See Section 4.5.2 for more information.

Here is a patches up-to-date rule example:

```
<xccdf:Rule
    id="xccdf_gov.nist.fdcc.xp_rule_security_patches_up_to_date"
    selected="true">
    <xccdf:title>Security Patches Up-To-Date</xccdf:title>
    <xccdf:description>Keep systems up to current patch levels
    </xccdf:description>
    <xccdf:check system="http://oval.mitre.org/XMLSchema/oval-definitions-5"
        multi-check="true">
        <xccdf:check-content-ref href="scap-win2000-patches.xml" />
    </xccdf:check>
</xccdf:Rule>
```

3.2.4.4 CVSS and CCSS Scores

SCAP 1.0 required the inclusion of static CVSS scores in XCCDF vulnerability-related rules. However, CVSS base scores sometimes change over time, such as when more information is available about a particular vulnerability, and CVSS temporal and environmental scores are intended to change to reflect current threats, security controls, and other factors. During scoring, current CVSS scores acquired dynamically, such as from a data feed, SHOULD be used in place of the `@weight` attribute within XCCDF vulnerability-related rules. Section 3.8 contains additional requirements for CVSS usage.

CCSS scores are more stable than CVSS scores, but they still may change over time. Accordingly, during scoring, current CCSS scores acquired dynamically, such as from a data feed, MAY be used in place of the @weight attribute within XCCDF configuration setting-related rules. Section 3.9 contains additional requirements for CCSS usage.

3.2.5 The <xccdf:Value> Element

Use of the <xccdf:source>, <xccdf:complex-value>, and <xccdf:complex-default> elements within the <xccdf:Value> element SHALL NOT be allowed. Within the <xccdf:choices> element of the <xccdf:Value> element, use of the <xccdf:complex-choice> element SHALL NOT be allowed.

One or more <xccdf:check-export> elements MAY be used to define the binding of <xccdf:Value> elements to OVAL variables. The format of the <xccdf:check-export> element is:

```
<xccdf:check-export value-id="XCCDF_Value_id"
    export-name="OVAL_External_Variable_id" />
```

The following <xccdf:check> element example demonstrates the use of this convention:

```
<xccdf:check system="http://oval.mitre.org/XMLSchema/oval-definitions-5">
    <xccdf:check-export value-id="xccdf_gov.nist.fdcc.xp_value_NoSlowLink"
    export-name="oval:gov.nist.fdcc.xp:var:66711" />
    <xccdf:check-export value-id="xccdf_gov.nist.fdcc.xp_value_NoBackgroundPolicy"
    export-name="oval:gov.nist.fdcc.xp:var:66712" />
    <xccdf:check-export value-id="xccdf_gov.nist.fdcc.xp_value_NoGPOListChanges"
    export-name="oval:gov.nist.fdcc.xp:var:66713" />
    <xccdf:check-content-ref href="fdcc-winxp-oval.xml"
    name="oval:gov.nist.fdcc.xp:def:6671" />
</xccdf:check>
```

The type and value binding of the specified <xccdf:Value> is constrained to match that lexical representation of the indicated OVAL Variable data type. Table 16 summarizes the constraints regarding data type usage. Additional information regarding OVAL and XCCDF data types can be found in the OVAL Common Schema documentation[13] and the XCCDF specification [XCCDF].

Table 16 - XCCDF-OVAL Data Export Matching Constraints

OVAL Variable Data Type	Matching XCCDF Data Type
int	number
float	number
boolean	boolean
string, evr_string, version, ios_version, fileset_revision, binary	string

3.2.6 The <xccdf:Group> Element

XCCDF group extension SHALL NOT be allowed.

3.3 Open Vulnerability and Assessment Language (OVAL)

This section lists requirements and recommendations for using the Open Vulnerability and Assessment Language (OVAL) to express an OVAL component of an SCAP source data stream (see Table 12).

---

[13] http://oval.mitre.org/language/download/schema/version5.4/ovaldefinition/documentation/oval-common-schema.html#DatatypeEnumeration and
http://oval.mitre.org/language/download/schema/version5.3/ovaldefinition/documentation/oval-definitions-schema.pdf

While the default version[14] of OVAL used in SCAP 1.2 SHALL be OVAL version 5.10, SCAP content SHOULD utilize the earliest SCAP-supported version of OVAL that includes all required tests and is necessary to properly address the SCAP content's purpose or use case. This approach, often referred to as the "least version principle", allows SCAP content to remain viable over a longer period of time by enabling the broadest support within products, while reducing the content maintenance burden that would be required to maintain revisions of content for multiple specification versions. The minimum supported OVAL version for SCAP 1.2 SHALL be OVAL version 5.3.

Because SCAP 1.2 supports the use of multiple OVAL source data stream components, an SCAP content creator could choose to divide the OVAL Definitions into multiple components based on the "least version" of each definition. For example, if some OVAL Definitions only required OVAL 5.3 while others required OVAL 5.10, then the content creator could create one OVAL source data stream component for the OVAL 5.3 definitions and another for the OVAL 5.10 definitions. SCAP 1.2 also supports multiple types of OVAL Definitions within a single OVAL source data stream component; for example, a benchmark could reference OVAL compliance and vulnerability definitions contained in a single data stream component.

The version of any particular OVAL document instance SHALL be specified using the `<oval:schema_version>` content element of the `<oval:generator>` element, as in this example:

```
<oval:generator>
  <oval:product_name>The OVAL Repository</oval:product_name>
  <oval:schema_version>5.10</oval:schema_version>
</oval:generator>
```

If an `<oval-var:oval_variables>` element is used to carry variable values between an XCCDF processor and an OVAL processor, the `<oval:schema_version>` of the `<oval-var:oval_variables>` element SHALL be the same as that of the `<oval-def:oval_definitions>` element whose external variables are bound by the `<oval-var:oval_variables>` element.

Required values for the `@class` attribute of an OVAL Definition are as follows:

1. "compliance" if it represents a check for the system's configuration complying with policy requirements (for example, having the required value for a specific configuration setting).

2. "vulnerability" if it represents a check for the presence of a particular software flaw vulnerability on a system.

3. "patch" if it represents a check for whether a discrete patch needs to be installed on the system.

4. "inventory" if it represents a check for the presence of a product of interest on the system.

The following requirements apply to particular classes of OVAL Definitions:

1. For compliance class definitions:

   a. If an OVAL compliance class definition maps to one or more CCE identifiers, the definition SHOULD include `<oval-def:reference>` elements that reference those identifiers using the following format:

      ```
      <oval-def:reference source="http://cce.mitre.org"
      ref_id="CCE_identifier"/>
      ```

---

[14] The OVAL Language versioning methodology is available here: http://oval.mitre.org/language/about/versioning.html

The source attribute SHALL be defined using either "*http://cce.mitre.org*" (preferred method) or "CCE".

b. Definitions that are directly or indirectly extended SHALL be limited to inventory and compliance classes.

2. For inventory class definitions:

   a. If an OVAL inventory class definition maps to one or more CPE identifiers, the definition SHOULD include *<oval-def:reference>* elements that reference those identifiers using the following format:

   ```
   <oval-def:reference source="http://cpe.mitre.org"
   ref_id="CPE_identifier"/>
   ```

   The source attribute SHALL be defined using either "*http://cpe.mitre.org*" (preferred method) or "CPE".

   b. Definitions that are directly or indirectly extended SHALL be limited to the inventory class.

3. For patch class definitions:

   a. If an OVAL patch class definition is associated with a source specific identifier (for example, Knowledge Base numbers for Microsoft patches), these identifiers SHOULD be included in *<oval-def:reference>* elements contained by the definition. For example:

   ```
   <oval-def:reference source="www.microsoft.com/Patch"
   ref_id="KB912919"/>
   ```

   b. If an OVAL patch class definition maps to one or more CVE identifiers, the definition MAY include *<oval-def:reference>* elements that reference those identifiers using the following format:

   ```
   <oval-def:reference source="http://cve.mitre.org"
   ref_id="CVE_identifier"/>
   ```

   This recommendation is weaker than its counterparts for the other class definition types because a CVE identifier is not an identifier for a patch; it is more of an association. For example, one patch could fix multiple vulnerabilities, so it would map to multiple CVE identifiers.

   The source attribute SHALL be defined using either "*http://cve.mitre.org*" (preferred method) or "CVE".

   c. Definitions that are directly or indirectly extended SHALL be limited to inventory and patch classes.

4. For vulnerability class definitions:

   a. If an OVAL vulnerability class definition maps to one or more CVE identifiers, the definition SHOULD include *<oval-def:reference>* elements that reference those identifiers using the following format:

   ```
   <oval-def:reference source="http://cve.mitre.org"
   ref_id="CVE_identifier"/>
   ```

The source attribute SHALL be defined using either "*http://cve.mitre.org*" (preferred method) or "CVE".

b. Definitions that are directly or indirectly extended SHALL be limited to inventory and vulnerability classes.

3.4   Open Checklist Interactive Language (OCIL)

This section lists recommendations for using the Open Checklist Interactive Language (OCIL) to express an OCIL component of an SCAP source data stream (see Table 12).

OCIL content SHOULD be used for checking rules that cannot be fully automated with OVAL. For example, a particular software product may not have an application programming interface (API) that supports OVAL use. Another example is performing a check that requires user interaction, such as asking the user to look up information within a management console or to report a serial number affixed to a computing device. OCIL can also be used to collect a user's own information, such as whether the user participated in a recent security training session.

If an `<ocil:questionnaire>` element maps to one or more CCE, CVE, and/or CPE identifiers, it SHOULD include `<ocil:reference>` elements that reference those identifiers using the corresponding following format:

```
<ocil:reference href="http://cce.mitre.org">CCE_identifier</ocil:reference>

<ocil:reference href="http://cve.mitre.org">CVE_identifier</ocil:reference>

<ocil:reference href="http://cpe.mitre.org">CPE_identifier</ocil:reference>
```

3.5   Common Platform Enumeration (CPE)

This section lists requirements and recommendations for using Common Platform Enumeration (CPE) to express a CPE component of an SCAP source data stream (see Table 12).

The Official CPE Dictionary data feed[15] MAY be used by SCAP components to reference CPE names. If use of the Official CPE Dictionary is impractical, a subset of the dictionary MAY be used instead. Creating the reduced official dictionary involves first identifying every CPE in `<xccdf:platform>` and `<cpe2:fact-ref>` elements contained within referenced `<cpe2:platform-specification>` elements in every benchmark in the data stream. Then these CPEs MUST be matched against every entry in the Official CPE Dictionary using the CPE name matching algorithm [CPE-M]. All CPEs matched in the official dictionary with a result of EQUAL or SUPERSET MUST be included in the reduced official dictionary.

One or more third-party dictionaries MAY be included in a data stream as well. All such third-party dictionaries SHOULD follow the requirements of the CPE Dictionary specification [CPE-D]. If including an entire third-party dictionary is impractical, a subset of the dictionary MAY be used instead. The reduced dictionary MUST be created using the same procedure outlined for creating a subset of the official dictionary.

In all cases, a dictionary component MAY be remote to the data stream collection.

Each CPE name [CPE-N] in an `<xccdf:platform>` or `<cpe2:fact-ref>` element within an XCCDF document SHALL match at least one CPE entry in a dictionary referenced by the data stream. A match is considered an EQUAL or SUPERSET result when matching the CPE name to a dictionary entry,

---

[15]   The Official CPE Dictionary is located at http://nvd.nist.gov/cpe.cfm.

as defined in the CPE Name Matching specification [CPE-M]. Only non-deprecated names SHOULD be used.

Checklist authors SHOULD ensure that each CPE name [CPE-N] they specify in an `<xccdf:platform>` or `<cpe2:fact-ref>` element within an XCCDF document has a check associated with its CPE name. If a corresponding check does not exist, then it will not be possible to fully detect the presence of the product and determine platform applicability. Because there may be a lag between the time that a new product is available and the Official CPE Dictionary is updated to include a CPE name for that product, third-party dictionaries would need to be used to compensate for the lag.

[CPE-D] provides the defining structure of a CPE dictionary. A `<cpe2_dict:cpe-item>` element MAY contain one or more `<cpe2-dict:check>` elements that reference OVAL inventory class definitions using the following format:

```
<cpe2_dict:check system="http://oval.mitre.org/XMLSchema/oval-definitions-5"
      [href="oval_URL"]>oval_inventory_definition_id</cpe2_dict:check>
```

For example:

```
<cpe2_dict:cpe-list xmlns="http://cpe.mitre.org/dictionary/2.0"
         xmlns:cpe2_dict="http://cpe.mitre.org/dictionary/2.0">
   <cpe2_dict:cpe-item
      name="cpe:/a:sun:java_system_messaging_server:6.2:-:sparc">
      <cpe2_dict:title>Sun Java System Messaging Server 6.2 sparc</title>
      <cpe2_dict:check
          system=http://oval.mitre.org/XMLSchema/oval-definitions-5
          href="example-sunjavamsg62-oval.xml">oval:org.mitre.oval:def:128
      </cpe2_dict:check>
      <cpe2-dict-ext:cpe23-item
      name="cpe:2.3:a:sun:java_system_messaging_server:6.2:-:-:-:-:-:sparc:-"/>
   </cpe2_dict:cpe-item>
</cpe2_dict:cpe-list>
```

The referenced OVAL inventory class definition SHALL specify the technical procedure for determining whether or not a specific target asset is an instance of the CPE name specified by the `<cpe2_dict:cpe-item>` element. This usage is encouraged for CPE components.

When creating a subset of the Official CPE Dictionary or a third-party dictionary, a `<cpe2_dict:check>` element on an entry MAY be added or modified if the existing check does not provide satisfactory content to test the presence of the CPE name.

If a `<cpe2_dict:cpe-item>` element contained in a CPE component references an OVAL inventory class definition, then that definition SHALL be resolved by an `@href` attribute referencing an OVAL source data stream component in the same data stream.

3.6   Common Configuration Enumeration (CCE)

To maintain consistency and accuracy, SCAP content referencing a configuration setting SHALL use the official CCE identifier if a CCE entry for a particular configuration setting exists in the official CCE list. If no CCE entry exists for the configuration setting of interest, the content author SHOULD seek to have a CCE identifier issued for the configuration setting. See the OVAL compliance class definition requirements in Section 3.3 and the `<xccdf:ident>` requirements in Section 3.2.4.1 for additional requirements involving CCE identifier references.

The current official CCE list is available at http://cce.mitre.org/lists/cce_list.html and new CCEs can be requested from the CCE Content Team. Submitters should review the information provided at http://cce.mitre.org/lists/creation_process.html regarding CCE core concepts and design constraints before submitting proposals for new CCE entries.

Use of an official, dynamic data feed is preferred to static coding of CCE-related supporting information in SCAP data sources. For example, NVD provides a data feed[16] that is the authoritative mapping between CCE identifiers and the control identifiers defined in NIST SP 800-53. Embedding control identifiers within SCAP content is strongly discouraged due to the maintenance burden that it imposes on content maintainers when the control identifiers are revised. A preferred technique is to embed only the CCE identifiers within SCAP content; when mappings to NIST SP 800-53 control identifiers are needed, dynamically acquire them from the official data feed and associate them to the SCAP content based on its embedded CCE identifiers.

3.7 Common Vulnerabilities and Exposures (CVE)

CVE references in SCAP content MAY include both "candidate" and "entry" status identifiers. Deprecated CVE identifiers SHALL NOT be used.

If a CVE identifier exists for a particular vulnerability, the official CVE identifier SHALL be used. If no CVE exists for the software flaw, an alternate identifier MAY be used, but the user SHOULD seek to have a CVE identifier issued for the vulnerability. The process for submitting unpublished vulnerabilities and obtaining CVE identifiers is available at http://cve.mitre.org/cve/obtain_id.html.

NIST provides a CVE data feed to support dynamic and current vulnerability information and associated metadata (e.g., CVSS values). The current schema is available at http://nvd.nist.gov/download.cfm.

3.8 Common Vulnerability Scoring System (CVSS)

The NIST CVE data feed, discussed in Section 3.7, is one source of CVSS base score and vector data that MAY be used by products to support additional use cases built on SCAP usage. In support of these additional use cases, CVSS base scores and vectors from this data feed MAY be used by products along with temporal and environmental scores and vectors from other sources.

3.9 Common Configuration Scoring System (CCSS)

CCSS base, temporal, and environmental scores and vectors MAY be used by products. Adopters of CCSS should be aware that it has significant differences from CVSS. Unlike CVSS data, which can be used by itself to aid in prioritizing vulnerability remediation efforts, CCSS data is not directly useful in the same way. Instead, CCSS data needs to be considered in the context of each organization's security policies and in the context of dependencies among vulnerabilities. See [CCSS] for additional information.

3.10 XML Digital Signature

Digitally signing source data streams is important to ensuring the integrity and trustworthiness of legitimate content, while preventing rogue content from being executed. Leveraging the Trust Model for Security Automation Data (TMSAD) specification [TMSAD] for SCAP can improve the legitimacy of authoritative content and create a more secure environment. As such, content authors MAY digitally sign source content following the guidelines in [TMSAD], along with the following requirements.

One or more XML digital signatures MAY be included as the last elements in the SCAP source data stream collection root element. Each signature MUST be represented as a `<dsig:Signature>` element and follow the W3C recommendation [DSIG]. Each `<dsig:Signature>` element MUST sign only one data stream.

---

[16]   http://nvd.nist.gov/cce.cfm

The *<dsig:Signature>* element MUST follow the recommendations in [TMSAD] and these additional requirements:

1. A *<dsig:Manifest>* element MUST be included within the *<dsig:Signature>* element as a *<dsig:Object>* element. The *<dsig:Manifest>* element MUST have a *<dsig:Reference>* element for each local component referenced by the data stream being signed. External components MAY be omitted from the *<dsig:Manifest>* element. Each *<dsig:Reference>* element referencing a *<ds:component>* or *<ds:extended-component>* element MUST point to the component being signed by identifying the component in the *@URI* attribute using "#" + *@Id* of the component.

2. A *<dsig:SignatureProperties>* element MUST be included within the *<dsig:Signature>* element as a *<dsig:Object>* element. At least one *<dsig:SignatureProperty>* element MUST be populated with *<dt:signature-info>* as specified in [TMSAD].

3. The first *<dsig:Reference>* element in a *<dsig:Signature>* element MUST be to the *<ds:data-stream>* element being signed. The *<ds:data-stream>* element MUST be referenced in the *@URI* attribute using "#" + *@Id* of the *<ds:data-stream>* element.

4. The second *<dsig:Reference>* element in a *<dsig:Signature>* element MUST be to the *<dsig:SignatureProperties>* element captured in a *<dsig:Object>* element within the *<dsig:Signature>* element. The *<dsig:SignatureProperties>* element MUST be referenced in the *@URI* attribute using "#" + *@Id* of the *<dsig:SignatureProperties>* element.

5. The third *<dsig:Reference>* element MUST be to the *<dsig:Manifest>* element captured in a *<dsig:Object>* element with the *<dsig:Signature>* element. The *<dsig:Manifest>* element MUST be referenced in the *@URI* attribute using "#" + *@Id* attribute of the *<dsig:Manifest>* element.

6. *<dsig:Reference>* elements on the *<dsig:Manifest>* element SHOULD be in the same order as the *<ds:component-ref>* elements on the data stream being signed.

7. Key information SHOULD be provided on the *<dsig:Signature>* element.

4. SCAP Content Processing Requirements and Recommendations

This section defines the processing requirements that SCAP content consumers MUST follow in order to correctly process SCAP 1.2 content. This section also provides recommendations that are not mandatory; organizations are encouraged to adopt them to promote stronger interoperability and greater consistency. The topics covered in the first part of this section are legacy support, source data streams, and XCCDF processing. The end of the section covers result-related topics: SCAP result data streams, XCCDF results, OVAL results, OCIL results, and result data stream signing.

4.1 Legacy Support

Content consumers supporting SCAP 1.2 SHALL process SCAP 1.2 content and SCAP 1.0 content. Content consumers SHALL process SCAP content as defined under the corresponding version of NIST SP 800-126 (for SCAP 1.2, this revision; for SCAP 1.0, the original release).[17] Content consumers that process legacy SCAP content MUST be capable of outputting results in the same SCAP version as the source content, and MAY convert the legacy SCAP results into SCAP 1.2 results.

Within the SCAP component specifications, certain constructs may be deprecated.[18] SCAP content consumers MUST support all deprecated constructs because they are still valid. This requirement ensures that legacy content that made use of these deprecated constructs continues to be supported.

Content consumers supporting OVAL SHALL support OVAL Definition documents written against OVAL versions 5.3, 5.4, 5.5, 5.6, 5.7, 5.8, 5.9, and 5.10.

4.2 Source Data Streams

Content consumers SHALL be capable of validating SCAP content against the appropriate schemas and Schematron stylesheets, detecting and reporting errors, and failing gracefully if there are errors. The relevant XML schemas are located at http://scap.nist.gov/revision/1.2/#schema, and the relevant Schematron rule sets at http://scap.nist.gov/revision/1.2/#schematron. See Section 3.1 for additional information on the Schematron rule sets.

Content consumers SHOULD validate XML digital signatures if they exist in the content. Validating a signature includes confirming that the signature value is valid, all of the reference hashes in the signature and manifest are correct, and the public key used to verify the signature is from a trusted source. A data stream with a signature that does not validate SHOULD NOT be evaluated by a content consumer.

Whenever a `<ds:extended-component>` that is not recognized by the tool is referenced from a `<ds:data-stream>`, `<ds:component>`, or `<ds:extended-component>` element, the tool SHALL issue a warning.

If more than one `<ds:data-stream>` element is specified on the `<ds:data-stream-collection>`, the ID of the `<ds:data-stream>` to execute MUST be indicated to the content consumer, and the content consumer MUST use the specified `<ds:data-stream>`. If more than one `<xccdf:Benchmark>` is referenced by a `<ds:data-stream>`, the ID of the `<xccdf:Benchmark>` to execute MUST be indicated to the content consumer, and the content consumer MUST process the indicated `<xccdf:Benchmark>`. Because SCAP and its component specifications do not formally define how to designate a particular data stream, benchmark, etc. in these cases, it is expected that products will implement these capabilities in a proprietary way.

---

[17] http://csrc.nist.gov/publications/PubsSPs.html#800-126
[18] The OVAL Language Deprecation policy is available here: http://oval.mitre.org/language/about/deprecation.html

4.3 XCCDF Processing

The following requirements and recommendations pertain to content consumers processing XCCDF benchmark and tailoring components from an SCAP source data stream.

4.3.1 CPE Applicability Processing

CPEs referenced in an *<xccdf:platform>* element directly or by a *<cpe2:fact-ref>* contained within a referenced *<cpe2:platform-specification>* element SHALL be evaluated as follows to determine their presence on a machine:

1. The CPE SHALL be matched against all CPEs in all of the dictionaries referenced by the *<ds:data-stream>* element. All CPEs that return an EQUAL or SUPERSET result as defined in CPE Name Matching [CPE-M] SHALL be used in evaluating the *<xccdf:platform>* or *<cpe2:fact-ref>*.

2. Either a list of CPEs found on the target asset MUST be known before the scan, or a list SHALL be generated. If a previously known list is used, it MUST be equivalent to a newly generated list. To generate the list, the *<cpe2_dict:check>* element data associated with the found *<cpe2_dict:cpe-item>* elements SHALL be evaluated against the target using the referenced OVAL inventory class definition. If a *<cpe2_dict:check>* returns "pass", then the corresponding CPE SHALL be added to the list of CPEs found on the target.

3. The list of CPEs found on the target asset, along with the *<xccdf:platform>* or *<cpe2:platform-specification>* SHALL be used as input to the CPE Applicability Language [CPE-L] algorithm to determine the XCCDF Benchmark applicability to the target asset.

4.3.2 Check System Usage

If an XCCDF component has multiple *<xccdf:check-content-ref>* elements, then check processing SHALL be performed according to [XCCDF:7.2.3.5.1] with the following changes:

1. For each *<xccdf:check-content-ref>* element, a content consumer either MUST attempt to retrieve the document referenced by the *<ds:component-ref>* element that is referenced directly by the *<xccdf:check-content-ref>* element's *@href* attribute, or it MUST resolve the *@href* attribute within the context of the XML Catalog specified as part of the *<ds:component-ref>* element used to reference this benchmark. If not resolvable, the next available *<xccdf:check-content-ref>* element SHALL be evaluated. If none of the *<xccdf:check-content-ref>* elements are resolvable, then the result of the rule evaluation SHALL be the XCCDF "notchecked" status and processing of the check SHALL end.

2. Once a resolvable *<xccdf:check-content-ref>* element is found, then check system processing SHALL proceed. When evaluating a rule, an *<xccdf:rule-result/xccdf:message>* with the *@severity* attribute value of "info" SHALL be generated, indicating the *<xccdf:check-content-ref>* *@href* attribute and *@name* attribute, if provided.

Content consumers SHALL implement check systems supported by SCAP as defined in Section 3.2.4.2. Content consumers MAY implement check systems that are not supported by SCAP. If a tool encounters a check system it does not support, it MUST issue a warning and it MUST continue processing according to the [XCCDF] specification.

When processing a patches-up-to-date rule, only OVAL patch class definitions SHALL be evaluated; all other classes of definitions (e.g., inventory class definitions) SHALL NOT be evaluated except when they serve, directly or indirectly, as criteria (extended definitions) of patch definitions.

4.4 SCAP Result Data Streams

An SCAP result data stream contains the results of the evaluation of one or more SCAP source data streams by an SCAP content consumer. The following requirements and recommendations pertain to content consumers generating SCAP result data streams.

An SCAP result data stream SHALL conform to the [ARF] specification. The following sections outline the details of the ARF report. In all situations, one or more component results (e.g., XCCDF, check results), the target asset, and/or the SCAP source data stream collection represented as a report request in ARF MAY be represented either as a local component in the ARF or as a remote resource, leveraging the remote resource capability built into ARF. This is a stripped down ARF example:

```
<arf:asset-report-collection>
   <rc:relationships>
       <rc:relationship type="arf-rel:isAbout" subject="xccdf1">
          <rc:ref>asset1</rc:ref>
       </rc:relationship>
       <rc:relationship type="arf-rel:isAbout" subject="oval1">
          <rc:ref>asset1</rc:ref>
       </rc:relationship>
       <rc:relationship type="scap-rel:checkContext" subject="oval1">
          <rc:ref>xccdf1</rc:ref>
       </rc:relationship>
       <rc:relationship type="scap-rel:fromSource" subject="xccdf1">
          <rc:ref>collection1</rc:ref>
       </rc:relationship>
       <rc:relationship type="scap-rel:fromSource" subject="oval1">
          <rc:ref>collection1</rc:ref>
       </rc:relationship>
   </rc:relationships>
   <arf:report-requests>
       <arf:report-request id="collection1">
          <arf:content>
              <ds:data-stream-collection>…</ds:data-stream-collection>
          </arf:content>
       </arf:report-request>
   </arf:report-requests>
   <arf:assets>
       <arf:asset id="asset1">
          <ai:computing-device>…</ai:computing-device>
       </arf:asset>
   </arf:assets>
   <arf:reports>
       <arf:report id="xccdf1">
          <arf:content>
              <xccdf:TestResult>…</xccdf:TestResult>
          </arf:content>
       </arf:report>
       <arf:report id="oval1">
          <arf:content>
              <xccdf-res:oval-results>…</xccdf-res:oval-results>
          </arf:content>
       </arf:report>
   </arf:reports>
</arf:asset-report-collection>
```

4.4.1 The Component Reports

The ARF report MUST contain a report object for each XCCDF, OVAL, and OCIL component executed when a source data stream is evaluated against a target. It MAY contain additional report objects for other results, such as `<oval-var:oval_variables>` or extended component results. Each component result MUST be captured as a separate `<arf:report>` element in the `<arf:asset-report-collection>` element, and when reporting on XCCDF, OVAL or OCIL, each component report SHALL use the element specified in Table 17 as its root element.

Table 17 - SCAP Result Data Stream Component Document Elements

Component	Document Element
XCCDF	`<xccdf:TestResult>`
OVAL	`<oval-res:oval_results>`
OCIL	`<ocil:ocil>`

Each SCAP result data stream component SHOULD NOT use any constructs that are deprecated in its associated specification. Validation of each component SHALL be done in accordance with the portions of this document that define requirements for the component. See Section 3.1.2 for more information on the SCAP Content Validation Tool, which can help validate the correctness of SCAP result data streams.

4.4.2 The Target Identification

The target asset MUST be represented in the ARF report using the `<ai:assets>` part of ARF. The `<ai:asset>` element populated about a target asset SHOULD include the fields specified in Table 18, where applicable.

Table 18 – Asset Identification Fields to Populate

Field	Location within Asset Identification Computing Device
Ethernet media access control address	connections/connection/mac-address
Internet Protocol version 4 address	connections/connection/ip-address/ip-v4
Internet Protocol version 6 address	connections/connection/ip-address/ip-v6
Host name	hostname
Fully qualified domain name	fqdn

Additional identification information MAY be captured in the `<ai:asset>` element (asset tag, system GUID, etc.) The guidelines specified in [AI] MUST be followed when populating the asset identification information.

Currently, only the target asset of the SCAP evaluation is identified.

4.4.3 The Source Data Stream

The source data stream collection that was used to generate the results against the target SHOULD be included in the ARF report as an `<arf:report-request>`.

4.4.4 The Relationships

Table 19 outlines the relationships that MUST be specified in the ARF report if the stated condition is satisfied.

Table 19 – ARF Relationships

Relationship	Condition	Cardinality	Definition	Subject	Object
arf-rel:isAbout	None	One for each component report	Each report is reporting about the asset	Component report	Target asset
scap-rel:checkContext	Benchmark report exists	One for each check component report (OVAL or OCIL)	Each check report is reporting in the context of the benchmark report	Check component report	Benchmark component report
scap-rel:fromSource	Report request exists	One for each component report	Each component report was generated from the SCAP source content	Component report	Report request
scap-rel:associatedWith	OVAL variables report is provided	One for each OVAL variables component report	Each OVAL variables report is associated with an OVAL result	Component report of OVAL variables	Component report of OVAL results

Figure 3 gives an example of how the resulting ARF report would look.

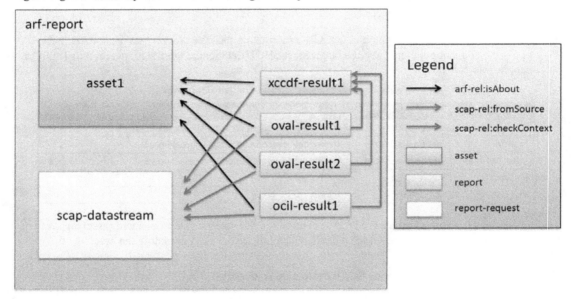

Figure 3 – Sample ARF Report Structure

4.5 XCCDF Results

The following requirements and recommendations pertain to content consumers generating XCCDF result data stream components.

Each XCCDF result data stream component SHALL comply with the XCCDF Results schema.

XCCDF test results SHALL be documented as the contents of an `<xccdf:TestResult>` element. To be considered valid SCAP result content, the `<xccdf:TestResult>` element SHALL meet the following conditions:

1. The *@start-time* and *@end-time* attributes SHALL be provided to indicate when the scan started and completed, respectively.

2. The *@test-system* attribute SHALL be provided, and it SHALL be a CPE name value indicating the product that was responsible for generating the results.

3. When the *<xccdf:TestResult>* is the root XCCDF element, then it will include an *<xccdf:benchmark>* element [XCCDF:6.6.2]. The *<xccdf:benchmark>* element MUST have an *@id* attribute specified.

4. Regarding the definition and use of *<xccdf:Profile>* elements, reported *<xccdf:set-value>* elements SHALL include all those values that are exported by the reported rules. The specific settings are those determined by the reported *<xccdf:Profile>*.

5. The *<xccdf:identity>* element SHALL identify the security principal used to access rule evaluation on the target(s). This will include the identity name or username used to perform the evaluation.

6. Each IP address associated with the *<xccdf:target>* SHALL be enumerated using the *<xccdf:target-address>* element.

7. An *<xccdf:target-id-ref>* SHALL be specified with a *@system* attribute of "http://scap.nist.gov/schema/asset-identification/1.1", an *@href* attribute value of "", and a *@name* attribute value of the ID of the *<ai:asset>* element in the ARF that this *<xccdf:TestResult>* is about.

8. The *<xccdf:rule-result>* elements report the result of the application of each selected rule [XCCDF:6.6.2]. The *<xccdf:check/xccdf:check-content-ref>* element SHALL record the reference to the check system specific result component report ID and check name within the result file using the *@href* and *@name* attributes, respectively. The *@href* attribute SHALL contain "#" + the *@id* of the *<arf:report>* containing the check result. This approach provides traceability between XCCDF and check results. Note that if *@multi-check* is not set to "true" and the *<xccdf:rule-result>* represents a group of checks, then the *@name* attribute SHALL be omitted. This is a stripped down example:

```
<arf:asset-report-collection>
  <rc:relationships>...</rc:relationships>
  <arf:report-requests>...</arf:report-requests>
  <arf:assets>...</arf:assets>
  <arf:reports>
    <arf:report id="xccdf1">
      <arf:content>
        <xccdf:TestResult>
          <xccdf:rule-result>
            <xccdf:check>
              <xccdf:check-content-ref href="#oval1"
                name="oval:gov.nist:def:2"/>
            </xccdf:check>
          </xccdf:rule-result>
        </xccdf:TestResult>
      </arf:content>
    </arf:report>
    <arf:report id="oval1">
      <arf:content>
        <arf:xccdf-res:oval-results>...</xccdf-res:oval-results>
      </arf:content>
    </arf:report>
```

```
        </arf:reports>
    </arf:asset-report-collection>
```

9. Where applicable to the target system, each of the `<xccdf:fact>` elements in Table 20 SHALL be provided. Previous versions of SCAP required additional facts; these have been incorporated into the use of the Asset Identification specification, as discussed in Section 4.4.2.

Table 20 - XCCDF Fact Descriptions

XCCDF Fact	Description of Use
`urn:scap:fact:asset:identifier:ein`	Equipment identification number or other inventory tag number
`urn:scap:fact:asset:identifier:guid`	Globally unique identifier for the asset, if assigned
`urn:scap:fact:asset:environmental_information:owning_organization`	Organization that tracks the asset on its inventory
`urn:scap:fact:asset:environmental_information:current_region`	Geographic region where the asset is located
`urn:scap:fact:asset:environmental_information:administration_unit`	Name of the organization that does system administration for the asset

4.5.1 Assigning Identifiers to Rule Results

The `<xccdf:rule-result>` element provides data indicating the result of assessing a system using the identified `<xccdf:Rule>` element. If the target `<xccdf:Rule>` identified by the `<xccdf:rule-result>` element's `@idref` attribute has one or more `<xccdf:ident>` elements with a `@system` attribute value listed in Section 3.2.4.1, then each `<xccdf:ident>` element SHALL also appear within the `<xccdf:rule-result>` element.

Here is an example for a CVE entry:

```
<xccdf:rule-result idref="java-upgrade-278" weight="10.0">
    <xccdf:result>pass</xccdf:result>
    ...
    <xccdf:ident system="http://cve.mitre.org">CVE-2006-0614</xccdf:ident>
    ...
</xccdf:rule-result>
```

If the `<xccdf:ident>` element is included, for tracking purposes it is important that produced XCCDF results have specific meanings. If an `<xccdf:ident>` element is present and it identifies a CVE, CCE, or CPE entry, then an `<xccdf:rule-result>` of "pass" SHALL indicate that the check content evaluated within the rule complied with one of the following:

- For a CVE entry, the target platform satisfies all the conditions of the XCCDF rule and is unaffected by the vulnerability or exposure referenced by the CVE.

- For a CCE entry, the target platform complies with the configuration setting guidance expressed in the XCCDF rule.

- For a CPE entry, the target platform was identified on the system.

It is important that these interpretations of `<xccdf:ident>` elements be preserved. For example, consider two policy recommendations. One is that a particular piece of software be installed, and the second that another piece of software not be installed. Both rules for these policy recommendations could use the same CPE entry in their `<xccdf:ident>` elements. However, because the interpretation of a

CPE entry is that a "pass" result indicates software was installed, the second policy recommendation's rule would violate this. This can be corrected by using the *@con:negate* attribute, a Boolean attribute that inverts the rule result. The second rule could check for the software being installed and then negate that result, thus giving a result consistent in meaning with the first rule. For rules that cannot have their interpretations preserved through the use of the *@con:negate* attribute, an alternative is to have a CCE entry corresponding to the recommendation. Rules that do not use *<xccdf:ident>* elements have no such restrictions.

4.5.2 Mapping OVAL Results to XCCDF Results

When evaluating an *<xccdf:Rule>* element that references an OVAL Definition, the *<xccdf:rule-result>* element SHALL be used to capture the result of this evaluation. This result SHALL be determined by evaluating the referenced OVAL Definition on a target host. The result value of an individual *<xccdf:check>* SHALL be mapped from the OVAL Definition result produced during evaluation. The corresponding *<xccdf:rule-result/xccdf:result>* value is then computed based on the result values of all relevant *<xccdf:check>* elements. (Normally only a single *<xccdf:check>* element is needed, but where an *<xccdf:complex-check>* element is used, there may be multiple results that must be combined, as outlined in the XCCDF specification.) While the OVAL specification permits limiting result status reporting, SCAP-conformant content SHALL include full status reporting, including Error, Unknown, Not Applicable, Not Evaluated, True, and False.

Content consumers SHALL apply the mapping illustrated in Table 21 when deriving *<xccdf:check>* results from OVAL Definition processing. The corresponding result value SHALL be recorded based on the *@class* attribute of the OVAL Definition where applicable.

Table 21 - Deriving XCCDF Check Results from OVAL Definition Results

OVAL Definition Result		XCCDF Check Result
error		error
unknown		unknown
not applicable		notapplicable
not evaluated		notchecked
Definition Class	**Definition Result**	
compliance	true	
vulnerability	false	Pass
inventory	true	
patch	false	
Definition Class	**Definition Result**	
compliance	false	
vulnerability	true	Fail
inventory	false	
patch	true	

The mappings in Table 21 are specific to each OVAL Definition class. For example, if an OVAL compliance class definition is processed and OVAL returns a result of "true", the content consumer is conveying the fact that the system was found to be compliant with that check and therefore returns a "pass" result for that check. A similar definition for a vulnerable condition will return results of "false" if that vulnerability was <u>not</u> found on the examined devices, resulting in a "pass" from the XCCDF check. Negations of check results or their combination in complex-checks may result in additional modification before the final corresponding *<xccdf:rule-result/xccdf:result>* value is known.

If the *<xccdf:Rule>* element under evaluation has an *<xccdf:check-content-ref>* element with the *@name* attribute omitted and an *<xccdf:check>* element with its *@multi-check* attribute set to "true", then the result of each evaluated OVAL Definition SHALL be recorded as a separate `<xccdf:rule-result>` element. In this case the `<xccdf:rule-result/xccdf:check-content-ref>` element SHALL identify the specific check result of each evaluated OVAL Definition using the `@href` and `@name` attributes as described in Section 4.5, item 8.

4.6 OVAL Results

The following requirements and recommendations pertain to content consumers generating OVAL result data stream components.

Each OVAL result data stream component SHALL validate against version 5.10 of the OVAL Results schema[19] regardless of the version of the OVAL Definitions document that was evaluated.

An SCAP OVAL result data stream component SHALL include the results of every OVAL Definition used to generate the reported results.

In order to be SCAP conformant, an SCAP content consumer SHALL be able to produce all the types of OVAL Results output described below. The specific result output SHALL be configurable within the SCAP content consumer.

In order to support SCAP instances where OVAL thin content (only the ID of the definition and the results) is preferred, SCAP content consumers SHALL support all valid values for the `<oval-res:directives>` controlling the expected content of the results file.

To support the ability for results to be consumed by the appropriate product(s), data results SHALL be expressed as Single Machine Without System Characteristics, Single Machine With System Characteristics, or Single Machine With Thin Results as follows:

1. Single Machine Without System Characteristics – A single result file that includes the results of all OVAL Definitions evaluated and "full" results types as described in the `<oval-res:ContentEnumeration>` element, without system characteristics.

   For this format, the values for the `<oval-res:directives>` element SHALL be:

   ```
   <oval-res:directives include_source_definitions="false">
       <oval-res:definition_true content="full" reported="true"/>
       <oval-res:definition_false content="full" reported="true"/>
       <oval-res:definition_unknown content="full" reported="true"/>
       <oval-res:definition_error content="full" reported="true"/>
       <oval-res:definition_not_evaluated content="full" reported="true"/>
       <oval-res:definition_not_applicable content="full" reported="true"/>
   </oval-res:directives>
   ```

   When creating the OVAL System Characteristics as defined by the `<oval-sc:oval_system_characteristics>` element, the `<oval-sc:collected_objects>` and `<oval-sc:system_data>` elements SHALL NOT be provided.

2. Single Machine With System Characteristics – A single result file that includes the results of all OVAL Definitions evaluated and "full" results types as described in the `<oval-res:ContentEnumeration>` element <u>and</u> the System Characteristics of the target evaluated.

   For this format, the values for the `<oval-res:directives>` element SHALL be:

   ```
   <oval-res:directives include_source_definitions="false">
   ```

---

[19] The OVAL schemas are described in detail at http://oval.mitre.org/language/about.

```
  <oval-res:definition_true content="full" reported="true"/>
  <oval-res:definition_false content="full" reported="true"/>
  <oval-res:definition_unknown content="full" reported="true"/>
  <oval-res:definition_error content="full" reported="true"/>
  <oval-res:definition_not_evaluated content="full" reported="true"/>
  <oval-res:definition_not_applicable content="full" reported="true"/>
</oval-res:directives>
```

When creating the OVAL System Characteristics as defined by the `<oval-sc:oval_system_characteristics>` element, the `<oval-sc:collected_objects>` and `<oval-sc:system_data>` elements SHALL be provided.

3. Single Machine With Thin Results – A single result file that includes the results of all OVAL Definitions evaluated and "thin" results types as described in the OVAL Results schema. A value of "thin" means only the minimal amount of information will be provided.

For this format, the values for the `<oval-res:directives>` element SHALL be:

```
<oval-res:directives include_source_definitions="false">
  <oval-res:definition_true content="thin" reported="true"/>
  <oval-res:definition_false content="thin" reported="true"/>
  <oval-res:definition_unknown content="thin" reported="true"/>
  <oval-res:definition_error content="thin" reported="true"/>
  <oval-res:definition_not_evaluated content="thin" reported="true"/>
  <oval-res:definition_not_applicable content="thin" reported="true"/>
</oval-res:directives>
```

When specifying OVAL system characteristics, a reference SHOULD be made to the target asset in the ARF report collection. Specifically, the `<oval-sc:oval_system_characteristics>`/`<oval-sc:system_info>`/`##any` SHOULD be populated with a `<con:asset-identification>` element. That element MUST be populated with a single `<arf:object-ref>` element that points to the `<ai:asset>` element in the ARF report collection pertaining to the OVAL result. See [ARF] for details on populating the `<arf:object-ref>` element.

4.7 OCIL Results

The following requirements and recommendations pertain to content consumers generating OCIL result data stream components.

An SCAP OCIL result data stream component SHALL include the results of every `<ocil:questionnaire>`, `<ocil:question_test_action>`, and `<ocil:question>` element used to generate the reported results.

4.8 Result Data Stream Signing

Digitally signing result data stream content is important to ensuring the integrity and trustworthiness of results. Leveraging [TMSAD] for SCAP can improve the legitimacy of results of SCAP content and create a more secure environment. As such, content consumers MAY digitally sign result content following the guidelines in [TMSAD], along with the following requirements.

One XML digital signature MAY be included in an `<arf:extended-info>` element in the ARF report. The signature MUST be represented as a `<dsig:Signature>` element and MUST follow the W3C recommendation [DSIG]. The `<dsig:Signature>` element MUST sign the ARF report collection root element.

The *<dsig:Signature>* element MUST follow the recommendations in [TMSAD] and these additional requirements:

1. A *<dsig:SignatureProperties>* element MUST be included in the *<dsig:Signature>* element. At least one *<dsig:SignatureProperty>* element MUST be populated with *<dt:signature-info>* as specified in [TMSAD].

2. The first *<dsig:Reference>* element in a *<dsig:Signature>* element MUST be to the *<arf:asset-report-collection>* element. The element MUST be referenced in the *@URI* attribute using the empty string convention "".

3. Two XPath Filter 2 transforms MUST exist on the first *<dsig:Reference>* element in a *<dsig:Signature>* element. Both MUST specify a filter type of "subtract". The first transform MUST specify the XPath "/arf:asset-report-collection/arf:extended-infos[count(arf:extended-info[dsig:Signature]) = count(*)]". The second transform MUST specify the XPath "/arf:asset-report-collection/arf:extended-infos/arf:extended-info[dsig:Signature]". In both cases, the namespace prefix "arf" MUST map to the ARF namespace specified in this document.

4. The second *<dsig:Reference>* element MUST be to the *<dsig:SignatureProperties>* element captured in a *<dsig:Object>* element with the *<dsig:Signature>* element. The *<dsig:SignatureProperties>* element MUST be referenced in the *@URI* attribute using "#" + *@Id* of the *<dsig:SignatureProperties>* element.

5. Key information SHOULD be provided on the *<dsig:Signature>* element.

In situations where it is desirable to countersign a result data stream (e.g., when a content consumer automatically signs a result data stream and then a person also wants to sign the results), the following requirements apply.

1. The *<arf:extended-info>* element containing the original signature SHALL be removed from the resulting document.

2. The original signature SHALL be captured as a *<dsig:Object>* element on the new *<dsig:Signature>* element.

3. The first *<dsig:Reference>* element on the new *<dsig:Signature>* element SHALL reference the *<dsig:Object>* element containing the original signature. The *<dsig:Object>* element MUST be referenced in the *@URI* attribute using "#" + *@Id* of the *<dsig:Object>* element.

4. The second *<dsig:Reference>* element MUST be to the *<dsig:SignatureProperties>* element captured in a *<dsig:Object>* element with the *<dsig:Signature>* element. The *<dsig:SignatureProperties>* element MUST be referenced in the *@URI* attribute using "#" + *@Id* of the *<dsig:SignatureProperties>* element.

5. A *<dsig:SignatureProperties>* element MUST be included in the *<dsig:Signature>* element. At least one *<dsig:SignatureProperty>* element MUST be populated with *<dt:signature-info>* as specified in [TMSAD].

6. Key information SHOULD be provided on the *<dsig:Signature>* element in accordance with [TMSAD].

7. The new `<dsig:Signature>` element MUST be placed in a new `<arf:extended-info>` element in the ARF report collection.

A signature that has countersigned another signature (also known as an enveloping signature) MAY be countersigned. When doing so, the requirements above SHALL apply to the new signature creation.

When signing a result data stream, the source data stream collection SHOULD be captured in the ARF report being signed.

5.   Source Data Stream Content Requirements for Use Cases

This section discusses additional requirements for the following SCAP-conformant content use cases: compliance checking, vulnerability scanning, and inventory scanning. Note that as stated in Table 3 in Section 3.1, each data stream is required to have a `@use-case` attribute in its `<ds:data-stream>` element with a value corresponding either to one of the content types defined in this section or to "OTHER", for data streams not corresponding to a defined use case. The required value for each content type is specified below in the appropriate subsection.

Each use case is subject not only to the requirements presented in this section, but also to all applicable requirements in Sections 3 and 4.

5.1   Compliance Checking

SCAP content can be used to compare system characteristics and settings against an SCAP-conformant checklist in an automated fashion. This can verify that operating systems and applications comply with security checklists and identify any deviations from those checklists.

The SCAP source data stream component that MUST be included for compliance checking is the XCCDF benchmark, which expresses the checklist. Each rule in the XCCDF benchmark SHALL reference one of the following:

*   An OVAL compliance definition. This definition SHALL be contained in an OVAL component, which holds definitions of compliance checks used by the checklist. An XCCDF benchmark's rules MAY reference one or more OVAL compliance class definitions in an OVAL component.

*   An OCIL questionnaire. This questionnaire SHALL be contained in an OCIL component, which holds questionnaires that collect information that OVAL is not being used to collect, such as posing questions to users or harvesting configuration information from an existing database. An XCCDF benchmark's rules MAY reference one or more OCIL questionnaires in an OCIL component.

*   An OVAL patch definition. This definition SHALL be contained in an OVAL component, which holds definitions for patch compliance checks. These checks may be needed if an organization includes patch verification in its compliance activities. An XCCDF benchmark MAY reference an OVAL patch definition through a patches up-to-date rule in a manner consistent with Section 3.2.4.3.

Each XCCDF benchmark SHALL have at least one rule that references either an OVAL compliance class definition in an OVAL component or an OCIL questionnaire in an OCIL component.

All OVAL components and OCIL components referenced by the XCCDF benchmark SHALL be included in the SCAP source data stream.

If the XCCDF benchmark component references any CPE names, then the SCAP source data stream MUST include a CPE component, which specifies the products or platforms of interest, and MUST include one or more OVAL inventory class definitions in an OVAL component that contain the technical procedures for determining whether or not a specific target asset has a product or platform of interest.

The `@use-case` attribute in the `<ds:data-stream>` element MUST be set to "CONFIGURATION".

5.2   Vulnerability Scanning

SCAP content can be used to scan operating systems and applications to look for known software flaws that introduce security exposures. The content enables consistent detection and reporting of these flaws.

The SCAP source data stream component that MUST be included for vulnerability scanning is the XCCDF benchmark, which expresses the checklist of the flaws to be checked for. Each rule in the XCCDF benchmark SHALL reference one of the following:

- An OVAL vulnerability definition. This definition SHALL be contained in an OVAL component, which holds definitions of vulnerability checks used by the checklist. An XCCDF benchmark's rules MAY reference one or more OVAL vulnerability class definitions in an OVAL component.

- An OCIL questionnaire. This questionnaire SHALL be contained in an OCIL component, which holds questionnaires that collect information that OVAL is not being used to collect, such as giving a system administrator step-by-step directions for manually examining a system for a vulnerability that cannot be detected with OVAL, and then collecting information on the results of that manual examination. An XCCDF benchmark's rules MAY reference one or more OCIL questionnaires in an OCIL component.

- An OVAL patch definition. This definition SHALL be contained in an OVAL component, which holds definitions for patch compliance checks. These checks may be needed if an organization includes patch verification in its vulnerability scanning activities. An XCCDF benchmark MAY reference an OVAL patch definition through a patches up-to-date rule in a manner consistent with Section 3.2.4.3.

Each XCCDF benchmark SHALL have at least one rule that references either an OVAL vulnerability class definition in an OVAL component or an OCIL questionnaire in an OCIL component.

All OVAL components and OCIL components referenced by the XCCDF benchmark SHALL be included in the SCAP source data stream.

If the XCCDF benchmark component references any CPE names, then the SCAP source data stream MUST include a CPE component, which specifies the products or platforms of interest, and MUST include one or more OVAL inventory class definitions in an OVAL component that contain the technical procedures for determining whether or not a specific target asset has a product or platform of interest.

The `@use-case` attribute in the `<ds:data-stream>` element MUST be set to "VULNERABILITY".

5.3 Inventory Scanning

SCAP content can be used to collect information on the software installed on systems. One example of how this could be used is to verify that a group of systems all have required security software programs installed. This could help verify compliance with technical security control requirements. Another example is to collect software inventory data on devices that are not directly connected to the enterprise network, such as smart phones.

Inventory scanning can also be applied to collect information on the presence of software artifacts on systems, such as malware or characteristics of malware that indicate its presence. SCAP content authored for this purpose can be used to detect classes or categories of malware based on system state that may be common across multiple malware instances. For example, it is a common practice to reuse malware code, making modifications to address available detection methods, change propagation characteristics, etc. It is also possible to author content that detects a specific instantiation of malware. For example, hashing of files can be used to identify a malicious executable or library.

The SCAP source data stream component that MUST be included for inventory scanning is the XCCDF benchmark, which references the inventory checks and captures the results. Each rule in the XCCDF benchmark SHALL reference one of the following:

- An OVAL inventory definition. This definition SHALL be contained in an OVAL component, which holds definitions of technical procedures for determining whether or not a specific target asset has software (product, platform, malware, etc.) of interest. An XCCDF benchmark's rules MAY reference one or more OVAL inventory class definitions in an OVAL component.

- An OCIL questionnaire. This questionnaire SHALL be contained in an OCIL component, which holds questionnaires that collect information that OVAL is not being used to collect, such as posing questions to users or harvesting inventory information from an existing database. An XCCDF benchmark's rules MAY reference one or more OCIL questionnaires in an OCIL component.

The *@use-case* attribute in the *<ds:data-stream>* element MUST be set to "INVENTORY".

Appendix A—Security Considerations

Major security considerations for this version of SCAP include the following:

- **Confidentiality.** SCAP does not define any mechanisms for protecting the confidentiality of SCAP content or results. Organizations can add on such protections as they deem appropriate, such as encrypting results files that contain sensitive information regarding system vulnerabilities.

- **Malicious content.** While SCAP does provide mechanisms for ensuring integrity of SCAP content and verifying content signatures, SCAP does not have any features specifically for handling malicious SCAP content (benchmarks, tailoring files, etc.) At a minimum, organizations should generate signatures for their content and verify signatures on all content before using it to ensure that the content has not been maliciously altered. Also, organizations should not process content that fails validation, and for stronger assurance may choose not to use any content that has not been signed.

- **Security value of content.** It is outside the scope of SCAP's capabilities to make any assertions or assessments regarding the security value of SCAP checklists and other forms of SCAP content. People and organizations may determine security value through their own methods, such as applying checklists to test systems and evaluating the results of those tests, but SCAP itself does not have any way of ensuring the security value of its content.

- **Component security.** Be aware of security considerations of all of the component protocols, specifications, standards, etc. used by SCAP. SCAP does not impose any additional security requirements on these.

Appendix B—Acronyms and Abbreviations

Selected acronyms and abbreviations used in the guide are defined below.

API	Application Programming Interface
ARF	Asset Reporting Format
CCE	Common Configuration Enumeration
CCSS	Common Configuration Scoring System
CPE	Common Platform Enumeration
CVE	Common Vulnerabilities and Exposures
CVSS	Common Vulnerability Scoring System
DHS	Department of Homeland Security
DoD	Department of Defense
FISMA	Federal Information Security Management Act
IR	Interagency Report
IT	Information Technology
ITL	Information Technology Laboratory
NIST	National Institute of Standards and Technology
NVD	National Vulnerability Database
OCIL	Open Checklist Interactive Language
OMB	Office of Management and Budget
OS	Operating System
OVAL	Open Vulnerability and Assessment Language
PCI	Payment Card Industry
RFC	Request for Comments
SCAP	Security Content Automation Protocol
SP	Service Pack
SP	Special Publication
TMSAD	Trust Model for Security Automation Data
URI	Uniform Resource Identifier
URL	Uniform Resource Locator
XCCDF	Extensible Configuration Checklist Description Format
XML	Extensible Markup Language

Appendix C—Glossary

This appendix contains definitions for selected terms used within the document.

Component schema: The schema for an SCAP component specification (e.g. XCCDF, CPE, CVSS). Within this document, this term is distinct from "OVAL component schema", which is defined by the OVAL specification.

Component specification: One of the individual specifications that comprises SCAP.

Content consumer: A product that accepts existing SCAP source data stream content, processes it, and produces SCAP result data streams

Content producer: A product that generates SCAP source data stream content.

Globally unique identifier: An identifier formatted following special conventions to support uniqueness within an organization and across all organizations creating identifiers. See Section 3.1.3 for the conventions.

Result content: Part or all of one or more SCAP result data streams.

Security Content Automation Protocol (SCAP): A suite of specifications that standardize the format and nomenclature by which software flaw and security configuration information is communicated, both to machines and humans.

SCAP component: A logical unit of data expressed using one or more of the SCAP component specifications.

SCAP conformant: A product or SCAP data stream that meets the requirements of this specification.

SCAP content: Part or all of one or more SCAP data streams.

SCAP data stream: A specific instantiation of SCAP content.

SCAP data stream collection: A container for SCAP data streams and components.

SCAP result data stream: An SCAP data stream that holds output (result) content.

SCAP source data stream: An SCAP data stream that holds input (source) content.

SCAP source data stream collection: A container for SCAP data streams and components.

SCAP use case: A pre-defined way in which a product can use SCAP. See Section 5 for the definitions of the SCAP use cases.

Source content: Part or all of SCAP source data streams.

Stream component: A major element of a data stream, such as an XCCDF benchmark or a set of OVAL definitions.

Well-formed: An SCAP-conformant data stream or stream component.

Appendix D—Normative References

The following normative references are pointers to the specifications, schema, dictionaries, and other information that are required to implement the SCAP 1.2 components:

[AI]	Asset Identification	http://scap.nist.gov/revision/1.2/#ai
[ARF]	ARF	http://scap.nist.gov/revision/1.2/#arf
[CCE]	CCE	http://scap.nist.gov/revision/1.2/#cce
[CCSS]	CCSS	http://scap.nist.gov/revision/1.2/#ccss
[CPE]	CPE	http://scap.nist.gov/revision/1.2/#cpe
[CPE-D]	CPE Dictionary	http://scap.nist.gov/specifications/cpe/#dictionary
[CPE-L]	CPE Applicability Language	http://scap.nist.gov/specifications/cpe/#language
[CPE-M]	CPE Name Matching	http://scap.nist.gov/specifications/cpe/#matching
[CPE-N]	CPE Naming	http://scap.nist.gov/specifications/cpe/#naming
[CVE]	CVE	http://scap.nist.gov/revision/1.2/#cve
[CVSS]	CVSS	http://scap.nist.gov/revision/1.2/#cvss
[DCES]	Dublin Core metadata version 1.1	http://dublincore.org/documents/dces/
[DSIG]	DSIG specification	http://www.w3.org/TR/xmldsig-core/
[ERRATA]	SCAP 1.2 (SP 800-126) errata	http://scap.nist.gov/revision/1.2/#errata
[OCIL]	OCIL	http://scap.nist.gov/revision/1.2/#ocil
[OVAL]	OVAL	http://scap.nist.gov/revision/1.2/#oval
[RFC2119]	RFC 2119	http://www.ietf.org/rfc/rfc2119.txt
[TMSAD]	TMSAD	http://scap.nist.gov/revision/1.2/#tmsad
[XCCDF]	XCCDF	http://scap.nist.gov/revision/1.2/#xccdf
[XINCLUDE]	XInclude specification	http://www.w3.org/TR/xinclude/
[XLINK]	XLink specification	http://www.w3.org/TR/xlink/
[XMLCAT]	XML Catalog specification http://www.oasis-open.org/committees/download.php/14809/xml-catalogs html	
[XMLS]	W3C XML Schema	http://www.w3.org/XML/Schema.html

Table 22 lists the schema file locations (and Schematron file locations, when applicable) for the SCAP component specifications.

Table 22 - SCAP Schema and Schematron File Locations

Prefix	Schema Location	Schematron Location (if applicable)
AI	http://scap.nist.gov/specifications/ai/#resource-1.1	
ARF	http://scap.nist.gov/specifications/arf/#resource-1.1	Embedded in the schema
CPE Applicability Language	http://scap.nist.gov/specifications/cpe/language.html#resource-2.3	
CPE Dictionary	http://scap.nist.gov/specifications/cpe/dictionary.html#resource-2.3	
OCIL	http://scap.nist.gov/specifications/ocil/#resource-2.0	Embedded in the schema
OVAL Definitions	http://oval.mitre.org/language/version5.10/	http://oval.mitre.org/language/version5.10/
OVAL Directives	http://oval.mitre.org/language/version5.10/	
OVAL Results	http://oval.mitre.org/language/version5.10/	http://oval.mitre.org/language/version5.10/
OVAL System Characteristics	http://oval.mitre.org/language/version5.10/	
OVAL Variables	http://oval.mitre.org/language/version5.10/	
SCAP constructs	http://scap.nist.gov/revision/1.2/#schema	
SCAP source data stream	http://scap.nist.gov/revision/1.2/#schema	http://scap.nist.gov/revision/1.2/#schematron
TMSAD	http://scap.nist.gov/specifications/tmsad/#resource-1.0	http://scap.nist.gov/specifications/tmsad/#resource-1.0
XCCDF	http://scap.nist.gov/specifications/xccdf/#resource-1.2	

Appendix E—Change Log

Revision 2 Release 0 – 12 July 2011

- Complete draft specification for version 1.2 released for public comment.
- Made editorial changes throughout the document.
- Added the following component specifications to SCAP: ARF 1.1, Asset Identification 1.1, CCSS 1.0, and TMSAD 1.0. Updated the following component specifications from SCAP 1.1: XCCDF from 1.1.4 to 1.2; OVAL from 5.8 to 5.10; and CPE from 2.2 to 2.3. Added and revised requirements throughout the specification to use these component specification versions.
- In Section 2, rewrote the conformance requirements and defined "content producer" and "content consumer" terms.
- Section 3:
  - Added an SCAP source data stream subsection and a subsection on digitally signing source data stream content.
  - Added identifier use requirements for `<xccdf:Rule>` and `<xccdf:ident>` elements.
  - Added requirements for the `<xccdf:Value>` element.
  - Added requirements related to Schematron rules.
- Section 4:
  - Revised legacy support requirements for SCAP content and OVAL definition documents.
  - Added an SCAP result data stream subsection. Added source and result data stream requirements throughout the section. Also added a subsection on digitally signing result data stream content.
  - Added a declaration of the FDCC Reporting Format.
- In Section 5, added malware detection material to the Inventory Scanning use case.
- Updated the normative references.
- Added Appendix C (change log).

Revision 2 Release 1 – 28 September 2011

- Final version released.
- Made editorial changes throughout document, including extensive addition of cross references.
- Section 3.1 (SCAP Source Data Stream):
  - Improved explanations of source data streams; added XML example and updated diagrams.
  - Added `@schematron-version` attribute to `<ds:data-stream-collection>`.
  - Added `<ds:Tailoring>` element to `<ds:component>` (was previously being treated as an element of `<ds:extended-component>`).
  - Expanded the discussion of Schematron files.
  - Added conventions for globally unique identifiers for `<scap:data-stream-collection>`, `<scap:data-stream>`, `<scap:component-ref>`, `<scap:component>`, and `<scap:extended-component>`.
- Section 3.2 (XCCDF):
  - Prohibited use of XInclude elements in XCCDF content, use of the `<xccdf:set-complex-value>` element within the `<xccdf:Profile>` element, and use of XCCDF group extension.
  - Clarified use of `<xccdf:ident>` elements and added the `@con:negate` attribute.
  - Clarified use of `<xccdf:check-content-ref>` elements.
- Section 4.1 (Legacy Support):
  - Added explicit information and requirements regarding deprecated constructs in SCAP component specifications.

- Section 4.2 (Source Data Streams):
  - Added a Schematron requirement.
  - Clarified what warnings tools must issue for an unrecognized *<ds:extended-component>*.
- Section 4.3 (XCCDF Processing):
  - Clarified the CPE applicability processing requirements.
  - Clarified requirements regarding the use of check systems not supported by SCAP.
- Section 4.4 (SCAP Result Data Streams):
  - Added an ARF example.
  - Added an *scap-ref:associatedWith* relationship requirement for ARF reports.
- Section 4.5 (XCCDF Results):
  - Deleted several facts from the XCCDF Fact Descriptions table.
  - Deleted redundant requirements (present in the latest XCCDF specification).
  - Clarified processing of *<xccdf:ident>* elements and added the *@con:negate* attribute.
  - Removed the requirements for the FDCC XCCDF results format.
- Section 5 (Source Data Stream Content Requirements for Use Cases):
  - Removed the OVAL-only use case.
- Appendices:
  - Added a new Appendix A containing security considerations for this version of SCAP.
  - Added a new Appendix C containing a glossary with key terms.
  - Added a list of SCAP schema and Schematron file locations to Appendix D.